TATTOOS . . .

Telling the Secrets of the Soul

Allan Dayhoff, D.Min.

First Printing: 2016

ISBN 978-1-387-93483-6

Evangelize Today Ministries
PO Box 7297, Fairfax Station, VA 22039

Other books by author, Allan Dayhoff, Jr., D.Min. Church in a Blues Bar

Evangelize Today Ministries is an organized church, 501 (c)(3) non-profit, and a member of the Presbyterian Church in America.

For more information about our ministries, visit www.evangelizetoday.info.

Table of Contents

Foreword

I didn't have time for it. But my friend Tommy told me I had to meet Allan Dayhoff, so I said OK. When I arrived at the Starbucks in the Westin Hotel overlooking Tampa Bay, I told myself and Al, "I've only got 45 minutes." Three hours later I was frustrated that our meeting had to end so soon. I felt like I'd made a new, and completely unexpected friend. Driving home I kept replaying the things we said. When I heard myself tell the story of our meeting to my wife, it hit me how significant this was. Not that I ever expected to see him again, but what we talked about continued to stir me.

Friendship takes hold of us and yanks us in directions we hadn't planned on going, but tattoos?

Everyone's soul holds its secrets. They mark our lives in profound ways. Whether they are noted on a calendar, are mysteriously buried in the gaps that fragment our family's hidden history, or, are intentionally written on the skin for the rest of the world to see, the sufferings of this life never ever go unnoticed by the soul. That's where we are indelibly marked.

"Tattoos" not only tells the story about Al Dayhoff's discovery of the effects of the secrets of the soul. It tells about the character of the researcher who made it happen. When I met him, I discovered a man who has been significantly gripped by the effects of the things that happen in people's lives as if they really matter, because they do! I think that his adventurous foray into the lives of people who wear tattoos has shed much needed light on the drama that everyone of us lives. And for this reason, his work is some of the most provocative I have seen in a long time. By really looking at, seeing and listening to people Al helps us understand just how profound life is, and how poignant each soul is. You are going to rediscover some of what you already know, but in a new way, through the lens of a tattoo—that despite being laced with suffering and tragedy, life is good, it is right, it is beautiful, it is worth living. The accounts and insights in these pages will move you to consider the purpose and character of your own life. I hope you'll treasure the person you find along the way.

When Al asked me to join this project I looked at him in disbelief. "Come on Al, that's not where I come from, it's not my experience." He looked at me with what I've come to appreciate is his impish smile that says otherwise. "Michael, there's some kind of genius at work inside you that gets this. You can do it. You already have." So, on that secure foundation I thought, why not?

An apocryphal quotation attributed to Mark Twain says, "The two most important days in your life are when you are born and the day you figure out why." Most of us are in some phase of the second day. Despite the many "Aha!" moments of insight anyone of us experiences, each one can become a stepping stone that takes us to another. For me, working on *Tattoos* has been exhilarating, frustrating, sometimes agonizing, but deeply refreshing, because I've been reminded to pay attention to the things I'd rather ignore, the things I overlook—like the ink on people's skin. Al's right — our lives and all that they consist of matter.

I hope the collaboration that has resulted in this edition of *Tattoos* is faithful to the stories it tells. And I hope that if it triggers any "Aha!" moments in you, you'll ride the crest of the wave for all you're worth, tumultuous as that might be, teasing you into the next chapter of discovery, whatever that is.

Michael A. DeArruda
Editor

Acknowledgements

As you'll see when you get into the body of this book, none of it could have come into being without relationships. I couldn't have told these amazing tales without the help of a very special team who came together to make this book possible.

First, to my partner in life Deb Dayhoff, a high school art teacher and professional potter extraordinaire: Your creativity, ability to format copy, and sound advice are only rivaled by your generous and patient persistence to bring things into being that weren't there before. You are simply amazing. You have seen into my soul and lovingly share this journey with me in spite of it.

Then there's Lennie Duensing. I believe that our chance meeting at my favorite blues bar in Florida, Ka'Tiki at Sunset Beach on the Gulf of Mexico had to be a divine appointment. Your keen insight, artful photography, and your kind researcher's heart have opened my eyes and heart to see many new images of the soul.

To Amy Loerch DeArruda, our silent but strong proofreader and advisor: How is it you have a lifetime of finely honed skill available just at this moment for this book to be published? Thank you for your unsung labors, dear friend.

To Michael DeArruda, a peer and advisor in the ministry: A lightning-bolt moment ignited something at a somewhat rushed, chance meeting. We finish each other's thoughts without speaking. Your hand in editing this edition of *Tattoos* has been life-changing for me. Your ability and willingness to venture into the unknown and sometimes uncomfortable has shown up again and again. I dearly hope this is just the beginning of a long relationship in researching and editing future books. Oh, by the way, did I mention the next project? Friend, we have 10 minutes left in this lifetime, let's get to this adventure. What do you say? Thank you for your masterful work.

To all of you, and especially to the many people from one end of the country to the other, who have welcomed me in to your lives, making mine infinitely more blessed. I thank you.

Allan Dayhoff, D. Min., Author
August 2018

With loving hands and heart, this tattoo artist begins applying her niece's first tattoo—a bouquet of flowers.

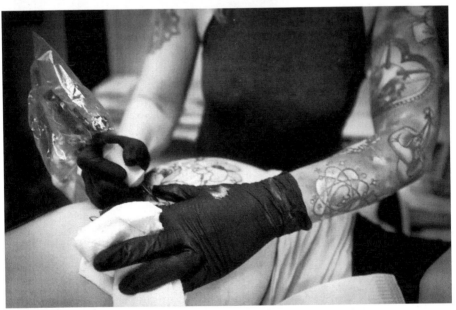

Preface

If a story is in you, it has to come out. —William Faulkner

The Little Thug at Airbnb

A new season started in Deb's and my life: We became Airbnb hosts. People from anywhere reserve one of our three spare bedrooms for one night or six weeks. We have a lot of guests who are the quick in-and-out, barely seen type. That's the way most like it.

But occasionally there is the casual unrushed soul who likes to talk with middle-aged empty nesters over an espresso in one of Deb's handmade mugs. There are some we grow fond of, and frankly hate to see go.

Jason came for one night. A Samsung phone executive in charge of something in their East Coast region. I invited him into my man cave on the deck: two leather seats, a copper-covered fireplace, a pagoda made of cedar tree trunks, and of course, cigars. He welcomed the offer.

All was going well—the usual lying and bragging about people, events, and evil forces we've conquered. We laughed as we kept one-upping each other with ever-more-improbable tales of derring-do. The first rule of the man cave is: All verification of the accuracy of any story, no matter how ridiculous, is strictly prohibited.

And then, it happened. A tattoo began to peek out from just below the arm of Jason's short-sleeve shirt. "I see a tattoo," I said, wondering what might come next. He immediately apologized and tried to pull his sleeve down, but it didn't work.

"It's a stupid tattoo I got when I was 15, OK? We all do dumb things."

I drew my cigar a little deeper, being sure to blow smoke all over him—a sign of affection in a man cave—which invited his counter attack, blowing a cloud that enveloped me. The second rule of the man cave is: The biggest smoke cloud wins. Jason had a vape machine, however, so his smoke clouds made mine look, well, small. Small is a very bad word between men. But I was on the offense, right?

His tattoo awaited explanation. So I waited, then waited some more. I wasn't disappointed.

"My buddy thought he could do a tattoo on me, so he drew a little guy with a gun, a punk in control of the world. It's stupid, a stupid tattoo!"

The image he hid that couldn't be fully covered I'd seen before, in the 70s. It looked like a teenager's attempt to draw the arrogant little thug with a shoe, bigger than the rest of his body lunging forward; he had a pistol in his hand. The more Jason talked, the more he told me what it seemed he didn't want me to know. But the little thug did.

Just in case I missed what he said, I waited. "Why stupid?" I asked.

"I was lost at 15. My mom died from an aneurysm and months later my dad died in a car accident. My grandparents took me in. It was a very kind gesture on their part. But they didn't take my younger brother. He was autistic, too much for them to handle."

Jason suddenly stopped. We both enjoyed a bit of cover in this awkward moment because the smoke that a cigar creates can cover a multitude of things—words, emotions, and truth. The longer the draw, the slower the exhale, the more timeless the moment can become. The smoke swirls, and your senses are focused on this ritualized pause. It's OK, no need to rush.

We took a while. I poked the fire. This was Jason's space. I wondered how he would use it. Maybe we had slipped from bragging into heart introspection too quickly, but, here we were.

Jason resumed. "My younger brother committed suicide, killed himself. My grandparents and all my relatives live in the wake of that pain, still." Once more I noticed Jason try to cover up the tattoo, like it was telling on him stuff he didn't want to reveal. He saw me catch his attempt.

"Stupid, stupid tattoo!" His repeated protest now seemed obligatory, half-hearted. I was sure that despite whatever embarrassment he might have, there would be another layer of disclosure tumbling out in a matter of seconds. And it did.

"I went to get it covered up, had an appointment with an artist, but on the very day of my appointment my grandmother died. So it's still here."

Jason is 33, but he sounded to me like an old blues man with a great blues song. He was telling his story, but it could have been sung.

"I've come a long way Al. I own a big house on a golf course. I'm getting married in the Bahamas next summer. I've got a good job. My fiancée is studying to be a psychologist," he paused.

"I provide her with a lot of material to practice on, but sometimes I just cut her off. It's a stupid tattoo of a little thug Al, right?"

My cigar puff suddenly rivaled his vape cloud. Maybe we were peers for a moment.

Jason couldn't help himself, "OK, OK! Maybe the little thug with a gun is a cautionary tale, something I can one day tell my son about. It won't bring back my mom, dad, or brother. But maybe the thug could help my son? Right, Al?"

I waited as he waited for me.

"Jason."

"Yeah, what?"

"I like your tattoo. That little thug is keeping the library of your life—your hopes, hurts, and mysteries. I think you're gonna start liking him in your forties."

Jason puffed and blew the biggest, and clearly the winningest smoke cloud at me. As the billow rolled over me we were both quiet.

Then, as if he'd suddenly seen himself in a new way, "Maybe you're right, Al."

"Peace, friend," I said.

Why tattoos?

Why would anyone write a book about tattoos? Aren't they the signs that social misfits wear as a badge that displays just how far out of the mainstream they are? And if they are out of the mainstream, what possible relevance could their weird body art have for my life? Aren't the poor souls who get themselves "inked" really just a contemporary version of sideshow freaks that we gawk at? I have to admit that once upon a time these were my assumptions about the people who wear tattoos.

So why write a book about tattoos? That's a good question—it's not as if I made a conscious decision to undertake a research project to study the strange and bizarre. It happened by accident. Or did it?

I spent 23 years of my life—the most robust period of my health and career—as a traditional protestant church minister. A lot of that time was consumed with establishing a congregation just outside the metro DC area. Even with the encouragement and institutional support of my denomination, creating a church community from scratch is a daunting task. From the beginning of the process I was convinced that this was a noble mission, that people needed a spiritual home, a community that would answer the profound questions we all face in this life, or at least offer them a place to wrestle with them.

Our little church grew from a small handful to dozens, and eventually hundreds of members. The culmination of what was my life's work—at least to that moment in time—was the erection of a multimillion-dollar worship center where hundreds of people gathered for weekly worship, education, and living a spiritually informed existence, grappling with who they were in relationship with God. It should have been the crowning achievement of my life.

But something wasn't right. At least, inside me something wasn't right. My inspiration had been to attract people to something new, something they hadn't seen or experienced before. Imagine my horror when I discovered that these efforts to create a new spiritual community wound up attracting people who had simply cycled out of their former church home and glommed on to ours! At our opening day dedication service, I looked at the packed sanctuary and realized that most of the people occupying the pews were not new to this at all. Like me, they'd been around the block a few times.

In fact, as we moved closer to moving our congregation out of storefronts and school auditoriums to a state-of-the-art campus, I made the sickening discovery that most so-called "church growth" in America is nothing more than a reshuffling of the same population that has been "doing" church for a long time. And our story was a carbon copy of that. Sure, there were some newcomers, honest-to-goodness first-time spiritual seekers. But most of the people filling the nation's churches are the same folks who have been there for decades. In our case, the dwindling congregations in our suburbs simply coughed up members who found the new thing in town that we were doing.

Almost as soon as our dedication service was over I intuitively knew the scripts of the thousands of conversations I was going to have with my staff and our members, and I didn't want to do that anymore. I had done more than two decades of church handshakes, church coffees, walking on church carpet, planning church budgets, picking out church songs for worship, recasting church talks that were politely received but didn't seem to penetrate to the level of real life that I was desperate to experience.

I couldn't pretend what I was feeling. I couldn't continue the exercise of recycling church folk. I was in crisis because what had given me purpose had now lost its ability to inspire me. I loved my people, especially the children. But I wasn't sure I could do this anymore.

Between my church and my home there's a blues bar. There couldn't have been a more unpredictable place for me to sit with my thoughts. But that's just what I did, over and over again. The longer I was there the freer I felt to come to terms with the disillusionment I was experiencing about the value and worth of the work I had done. But if the meaning of all that effort was evaporating, what would be left? Before I quite knew what was happening I found myself drawn to the people at the bar. Actually, it worked more like this—they were drawn to me while I was trying to hide out and examine my life. I chronicled this unbelievable saga in my previous book, *Church in a Blues Bar*.

This is where the tattoo adventure began. I didn't see it coming, because I went to the bar—like a lot of first timers probably do—to put some space between me and my career crisis. While I was sorting, something else was going on. I got comfortable in the bar and with its patrons. And before I knew what had happened or why, my curiosity about the people around me turned into genuine interest and care. It dawned on me: "I am theirs and they are mine."

To my utter surprise, when I saw the blues bar patrons as my parishioners, I cared about them, I *saw* them. I saw what they looked like: the color of their hair, the dullness in their eyes, and the ink on their skin. Not all of them have tattoos, but a lot do. And when I saw, really *saw* how people presented themselves, inked skin and all, I was equally shocked and embarrassed at my previous lack of attention to this detail. Here I am a minister who, as a professional people watcher, seeks to know and understand the stories that inform their lives. But I was totally unaware that better than 40% of today's population wears tattoos. How could I have missed this?

I believed that the meaning of a tattoo is consciously held by the person who wears it, that their body art is a decorative application whose message is known to its owner. Like the guy who wears a Chicago Cubs cap is letting the world know he's a fan. No need to ask. But what if there is more, far more to the tattoo's function? What if the tattoo is a tool that mediates a dynamic dialogue not simply between the wearer and those who see it, but between the soul and its owner, between the soul and its creator? As you'll discover in the stories told on these pages, tattoos may be two-dimensional, but they plumb the depths of the soul and human experience, defying dimensional limitation.

Tattoos are more than silly marks on people who can't go mainstream. Their history began almost 5,000 years ago. It includes Native Americans totems, African skin markings with geometric mud designs, and Polynesian tattoo art. In Western culture, tattoos are now becoming mainstream. But perhaps for the first time in history they are worn as an expression of personal identity.

The more I got to know the patrons in the blues bar, the more I got to know their human experience at levels that surprised me. Frankly, I've learned so much from the "conversation" with the tattoo—you'll understand what I mean by that—the more I have been drawn to the people who wear them, like a moth to a flame.

But why? I suspect that the people's hearts are sacred ground where the most important things any of us will ever discover can be found. We live and act out the grand dramas of our lives, most often unconsciously. In my conversations with the tattoo I've learned to cherish their owners, respect their profound experiences, and love them in a way that still startles me.

So far, the moth has not been extinguished. This book is the result of six years and 900 interviews to answer two questions: What are people writing on themselves, and why? I've prepared this second edition because I've had new encounters that have opened new insights about the tattoo phenomenon. I also see a connection between the inked stories that appear on skin and the undisclosed tales that lie hidden in every human heart.

In the original edition, *God & Tattoos*, I was attempting to discover whether there is a relationship between a universal human search for meaning, captured in the experience and notion of God, and the messages I saw on human skin. My conclusion is yes, that relationship exists. We'll talk about it in this book, too. But not every dramatic depiction of a person's story connects in a straight line to God. I have been humbled by countless moments of bearing witness to the significance of the events depicted in tattoos and their effects on the people who wear them.

On this journey I've traveled from back-alley tattoo parlors to huge tattoo conventions where thousands of inked people congregate. But burger joints, coffee shops, Walmart parking lots, churches, and junk yards have also turned up provocative encounters with tattoos and their owners. I've met people of every race, creed, size, age, and socioeconomic stratum. They are believers, atheists, and agnostics—but philosophers all, trying to understand their lives—an exercise that takes place with an eye on its boundary line, death. The themes of life and mortality constantly appear in tattoos.

In the final week before his death Jesus entered Jerusalem to the deafening cheers of an adoring throng. "Blessed is the king who comes in the name of the Lord! Peace in heaven and glory in the highest!" (Luke 19:38) But this eruption of adulation and worship was blasphemy to the religious authorities of the day. People were calling this mere mortal "God" and "Savior"! The ruling elders demanded that Jesus shut it down. "'I tell you,' he replied, 'if they keep quiet, the stones will cry out.'" (Luke 19:40) Ever wonder why? Because the truth cannot be silenced. It will leak out, it will cry out, it will scream out, it will paint and write itself out, no matter what.

In this era of human existence, especially as we witness the erosion of institutions that supported Western society's meaning and values, the soul is shouting out its truth. It's as if the image of God has become so desperate to speak that it can no longer abide the organs and vehicles of disinformation that seem to envelope our lives. Inked people have become living testaments by writing on the outside what is on the inside—even if they are not always conscious of the depth of their own soul's message.

I wasn't planning this journey, and neither were you. But then, that's a familiar pattern in life. We wind up in places, making discoveries, and understanding things we never knew before—or perhaps we do know at a level that is deeper than we dare risk going.

Join me on the journey. There's something that is yearning to be known. Can you see it? Can you read it? Can you hear what it is saying?

INTRODUCTION

I noticed Brutus in a blues bar in Manhattan, New York City. What a bruiser he was. He looked to be about fifty. His brazen, bold tattoos caught my attention and in that same instant fear gripped me. But every part of my brain hadn't fully processed the situation. I was stupid enough to not heed the obvious four-alarm warning his whole person was blaring. "STAY AWAY OR ELSE!" But I didn't.

Talk about contrasts—I had on a starched, white, button down shirt with nerdy glasses, and he was, well, like an angry grizzly bear who had just been disturbed from hibernation.

I managed to secure a spot next to him at the bar. I took my time, waiting for courage to appear. I didn't show up on cue. I went ahead anyway. "Excuse me. I like your tattoos. May I ask you a few questions?"

Either he didn't hear me or chose to ignore me. I thought about tapping him on the shoulder, then reconsidered. So, I waited. When he soon realized, this annoying fly wasn't going away he turned to me for the first time and barked, "What?"

I cleared my throat in a polite non-mocking way—maybe it was an unconscious reflex intended to let Brutus know that I understood the power differential between us. Impatient, he barked again, this time with more energy and force, "What!" Only then did I realized he was recovering from a massive hangover, from the night before, or maybe from his whole life.

I'd opened up this can of worms, so I had to start with what was right in front of me, "Sorry, man. You look like you had a rough night."

He eased up a bit. "Yah." We were now in a full-blown conversation! Empathizing with his immediate condition got him talking. Sometimes it's noticing the smallest, but most evident thing about a person, right where they are at that moment, that is the pathway to a connection.

Still groggy and a bit annoyed, he opened up to me, "What do you want to know?"

"You're saying something with your tattoos. I'm interested. Can you tell me?"

Brutus showed me the very first tattoo he ever got. It was on his shoulder and it was blurry, kind of like he was—tattoos tend to lose their crispness over time. It was a collection of martial arts symbols.

"For years I found my religion in the martial arts. Then, my body just broke from all the blows."

Next, he pointed to his forearm. There was a blurry rainbow. "This one is about the years of drugs and LSD I did."

Around his neck were rosary beads. "This is in honor of my mother." It was clear from what he told me, he was holding on to a thread of belief that the beads represented to him, a religious symbol that he draped on his body like a prayer that God would see some kind of plea from his heart.

Suddenly, Brutus stepped a bit away from the bar. Still wary of this bear-like character, I wasn't sure what he was doing. Then, in the middle of this tight, noisy crowd he ripped off his shirt. I was stunned! By what he did and what I saw. But nobody else reacted. Nobody noticed!

How many times does this happen? People say and do things, things that are intended to get a response and nobody notices. I couldn't help thinking this would be the most desperate of any condition I could imagine—to exist but not be heard, not be seen, not be noticed—invisible!

Brutus was a hairy beast of a man. In his post-inebriated condition he had no sense of shame. The tattoo tour continued. In the middle of his chest were three crosses, all with people hanging on them. The gruesome sight shocked me.

Looking up he said, "My hope in life was to move from being the self-righteous a**hole hanging on the left of Jesus, to becoming the thief on his right. I'm simply asking for Jesus to remember me." I was stunned. The beads on his neck DID connect with a prayer—a confession, a longing. Here was a guy who'd tried everything and still came up short, so he prayed, by wearing it.

I was overcome with emotion that wanted to explode out into the open like Brutus's life had right in front of me. "God bless you!" I heard the words tumble out of my mouth as if someone else said them. In the middle of a crowded bar, in one of the world's most congested cities, an anonymous fifty-year old man, whose body, mind and heart had been broken, opened a window into the deepest, most real part of himself. And it happened because someone simply noticed.

I was blown away. But what's more amazing? This was not a one off. To say I've been surprised that it happens a lot is an understatement. Perhaps you're skeptical, wondering just how much I've embellished what happened. I'm telling you—this is the truth. Not once, not occasionally, but a lot of the time. Why? In a world that is crumbling around us the soul is desperate to speak, to be heard, to be known, to be seen, and to matter.

I never know what's going to happen when I ask someone about their tattoo. Yes, some ignore me. But I'm finding that most, even people who won't allow themselves to be engaged, are wearing these markings because they cannot keep themselves stuffed inside anymore. Our souls are telling on us. It seems to me we can't hold them back.

Brutus put his shirt back on. Looking like a different person than the one who tried not to notice me at first, he smiled. We both nodded our heads like guys do when we want to telegraph something special has registered inside. And then, looking a little confused about what had just happened, he quickly left. I stood there, as if ordinary life had been suddenly peeled back for a moment to reveal a realm even more real than what I thought I knew. I'd been shown a naked, searching soul.

Some might ask why I didn't say something more, something to lift his burden, something to heal his brokenness. Honestly, I don't have the words, or the power, or audacity to presume I can do any of those things. Argue with me if you like—all I can tell you is that the encounter itself changed Brutus and it changed me. How?

He told me what he most needed to say and what he most needed to have someone hear. The unscripted blessing that leaped off my tongue told him "I don't judge you. I accept you. You are worthy of gentleness, kindness and mercy." As if to say, "Brutus, there are no accusers here who can keep you from what you long for—not even yourself. Go, and trust that one day you will be with Jesus, in paradise."

And me? I didn't deny my fear but neither did I let it dictate what I did. Yes, my goal was to interview an interesting subject to gather research about tattoos. But what I received was way more than that. I received the gift of an uncovered soul who wants to be noticed. There are some experiences that have such an effect on us, though we analyze and try to put them into words, will always mean so much more than we can fathom. For me, this will always be one of them. Tattoos are telling the secrets of the soul.

Chapter 1: The Canvas of the Soul

Life is a great big canvas; throw all the paint on it you can. —Danny Kaye

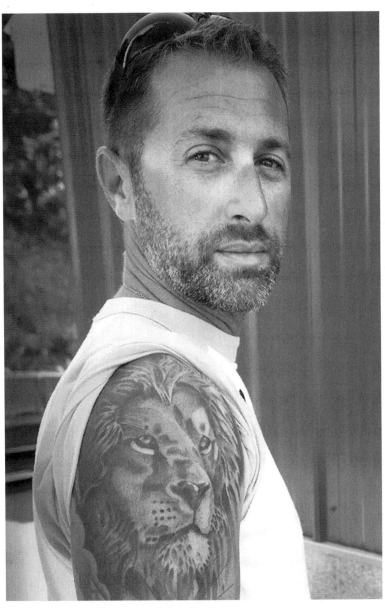

This father, husband, and baseball coach, says that many of his fellow Christian friends tell him that it's sinful to have tattoos, but he believes it's a way show God's glory, and a way to open conversations.

Nora Hildebrandt was America's first tattooed lady. She was a circus act with Barnum and Bailey in the 1890s. Her father Martin was the first professional tattoo artist in the United States. When he wasn't working on sailors and soldiers, he practiced his craft on his daughter's skin. Nora was eventually inked neck to toe with 365 unique designs. A grossly fabricated story designed to attract massive crowds of curious spectators explained that while being held captive by the legendary Lakota Chief Sitting Bull, father and daughter were consigned to a yearlong marathon of daily tattooing, accounting for the number Nora wore. Her fame was eclipsed, however, when "La Belle Irene" caught the eye of the circus industry. Irene Woodward used tattoos to tell the story of her beauty to a gawking world that was unfamiliar but fascinated with inked skin. Many other men and women seeking fame would follow these pioneers as celebrated sideshow attractions in America and Europe.

Like many things in contemporary culture that were considered public oddities a century ago, tattoos have now become commonplace. Still, many people—especially those in the older generations—are repulsed by them; many believe that tattoos are for sailors and thugs. Why permanently mark your skin with loud designs, gaudy pictures, and cryptic messages? If this is your predisposition, get ready to be surprised.

Now that our children and grandchildren are inking themselves, we're offended—and may even feel violated. After all, don't we have a legitimate claim upon the real estate of their bodies? We see a growing crop of fantastic images blazing across the necks, shoulders, chests, and arms of the next generation as we stare across the Thanksgiving table. But we can't *not* look. And we can't not conclude that something strange is going on—and we are being left out of it.

Maybe it's better to let our children live through their chosen fad. But permanent ink can't be a fad—it's permanent! We wonder if our youth realize that their tattoos might jeopardize the inevitable watershed moments they haven't had yet—dating, marriage, job searching, to name a few—not to mention their respectability. Or are they doing this to consciously disqualify themselves from the cycles of life we once took for granted? And if so, why would they consciously limit themselves?

If you harbor such concerns, I'm asking you to slowly wade into the encounters I've had and my observations about the meaning and experience of tattoos. This is a genuine invitation to listen as I tell you about my journey into an arena of human experience I once thought was marginal and of no deep significance. Nothing could be further from the truth.

I have no interest in selling you on the proposition that tattoos or either good or bad. Nor do I presume to make a definitive statement on their meaning. What I do hope is that the stories I tell and the observations I've made will lead to an appreciation of the indisputable fact that there is a lot more going on inside of people than we usually dare to learn. You might even find, like I did, that the tattoo phenomenon is nothing short of an MRI or CT scan of what may be going on in your soul, whether you wear a tattoo or not.

I hope you will move from a sideline observer of the unfamiliar and bizarre to an empathetic fellow sojourner. As you participate in the drama of these stories I hope your own questions will push their way to the surface of your awareness. I hope you will discover something about your own strength, gentleness, and precious worth, even in the midst of the torn, ragged, and frayed threads of your existence. Friend, we all have these.

If you wear tattoos I'd love to hear your reflections on the content of this book. I know that ten little chapters cannot fully describe every nuance and influence that put your backside into an inking chair while the secrets of your soul were penned indelibly onto your dermis. I hope you sense that I've tried to hear and learn from you.

I've learned that each tattoo is as different as each person's personality and life story. To my great delight and complete wonderment I've found many things inside and under your tattoos. I've experienced euphoric moments when you made your own discoveries about what was hidden underneath the ink. You taught me how to show respect and be patient. The secrets you've disclosed silenced the internal voice of my self-conscious preoccupation. I knew I was standing on holy ground. Your willingness to allow me to peer with you into the most sacred places has changed me in ways I can't even begin to explain.

When I first wrote about this journey, I'd conducted more than 300 interviews and spent weeks inside tattoo studios. That was 2016. You'd think I might have heard and seen it all by now. But every story, every person, every tattoo, every unexpected revelation has drawn me to the next one. Now, after nearly a thousand meetings, and God knows how many hours, miles, villages, cities, conventions, and towns, I am still taken by surprise with the amazing diversity of experience, broken dreams, and mountaintop ecstasies people have.

Yes, there is untold pain in the markings of lost and found loves, and heroic quests to be loved, by mothers, fathers, children, friends, soul mates, and God. I am quite literally blown away that human beings endure not just life events themselves—but the effects of them in our hearts, minds, and souls. No matter what condition any of us is in, the fact that we live is itself a miracle of unmeasured proportions and significance. I have come to treasure the gifts and curses of life in an entirely new way.

I love this adventure. Not in the shallow, ephemeral way we often speak of it. I am not a voyeur of what some might call the bizarre. This research is not so much about tattoos but what they have revealed to me: Tattoos are the portals to the souls of the people who wear them. Thank you, my friends for welcoming me again and again beneath the surface of your skin.

Soul talk

There may be many obstacles to human encounters, but with a small lighthearted exchange the rusty hinges of the heart turn and the door opens for the start of soul talk. Small country diners are among the places where I often find such doorways—and some pretty amazing food. If the way to a man's heart is through his stomach, I've learned a corollary: The way into a deep conversation is often over a great country meal.

I was in central Pennsylvania, driving along historic Route 30 in the late afternoon. This beaten path used to be the lifeline between Philadelphia and Pittsburgh, first by foot, then by horse, then rail, then automobile. Many towns along the way have road signs from another time, and hotels that have not changed since the 1960s. These establishments compete for customers and dignity. They all have a story to tell tourists and natives alike. The Gettysburg Battlefield, York's Barbell, and the Lancaster Amish buffets all beckon you in to look around, discover something new or old, eat, relax, and buy their trinkets. The traffic lights that repeatedly make you stop can be maddening, especially when you're in a hurry. But they can be a gift if you need a reason to slow down or to let your senses off-leash.

I was riding with a friend who likes to pay the restaurant bill. On cue, a rusting, silver-colored diner with work trucks parked outside caught our eye. We pulled in and sat down in a 60-year-old plastic laminated booth. People around us were talking about the new traffic light being put in nearby. The buzz was not favorable about the upgrade.

The waitress came over, a small-framed woman in her mid-thirties showing unmistakable signs of a hard life. Like the booth we sat in she had wear marks in all the expected places, but her simple beauty was evident too. Sort of like the sun trying to peek out from behind storm clouds. She handed us the menus while asking, "What can I get you boys?"

We told her, and she began to write our order. Then exasperated, she fumed, "These damned pens never work, you know." She wrote harder trying to get the pen to work, but gave up. "Just hang tight, I got this under control."

Before she'd turned away, as casual as asking for a cup of coffee, I said, "I like your tattoos, do they mean something?" Her reaction was one I've learned to see coming. She quickly tucked the order pad under her arm, put her fists up and mockingly barked, "Are you making fun of me?" Her gaze and stance were fun, serious, and fragile, all in the same instant.

Then she relaxed her hands. "They all have meaning," she said with a soft voice. I held my eyes on her and stayed silent in case she would venture to tell more about the story written on her skin. She pulled back her sleeve, pointing to her left shoulder. "These are the names of my two children." Then she paused to return the same still gaze, as if to say, "I can say more if you want me to." On her shoulder was a baby wrapped in a blanket, with just her tiny face showing below a name.

"And the baby?" I asked.

"I miscarried her in the eighth month, nine years ago. I don't want to forget her."

"I'm so sorry." What else could I say?

"It's okay," she returned.

Then came the complete show and tell. She pulled up the back of her shirt to show a poem written by her dead father. Then she tugged to lower the edge of her pants to reveal his face. Wide across her chest was a sunrise with Indian mosaic art that she said represents recovery from two divorces and a car wreck where she lost a kidney.

"Terry, we got customers!" came a voice from behind the counter.

She spun around and took off. "God Bless you, Terry, and God's gentle care on you," I thought to myself as Terry lurched back into the present to resume her work.

A casual question about an obvious picture opened a window into Terry's soul that transported us both to a place invisible to the confines of the diner. As she lifted her clothing to expose her skin, Terry peeled back the veneer of her six-to-noon life as a small-town waitress and revealed herself in another dimension, as a grieving daughter, mother, and wife who has been smashed and torn apart to the depths of her soul, now missing parts of herself, yet still walking and talking and serving others a full helping of reality mixed with a side of playful protectiveness that invites the true connoisseur of life to taste and savor what was being set before him.

As if admitting we'd just been invited to see behind a curtain few ever do, my friend looked over at me when Terry had gone and said, "By the way, Al, *you're* paying the bill today!"

Tsunami of change

On March 11, 2011, the fourth-largest earthquake ever recorded, at a magnitude 9.0 erupted off the northeastern coast of Japan, unleashing a historic tsunami that swept away everything in its path in a matter of minutes. Sixteen thousand deaths, 7,000 injuries, 2,500 people missing, and 400,000 buildings destroyed or damaged beyond repair. Another three-quarters of a million buildings were partially damaged. The 130-foot wall of water that slammed into the island caused catastrophic change to the nation's landscape, consciousness, and civilization. And who can forget the fear as we watched three nuclear reactors melt down at the Fukushima power plant? The World Bank estimates that at $235 billion, this was the costliest natural disaster in history.

The initial earthquake lasted up to six minutes. But the effects of the tsunami were staggering: A six-foot-high wave crashed into Chile and a fjord in Norway experienced boiling water and surging waves. Icebergs broke off of Antarctica. The tsunami deposited 5 million tons of refuse into the oceans; household items still wash up on the Pacific coasts of Canada and the United States eight years later. It's estimated that this massive quake shortened the day about 1.8 microseconds by shifting the Earth's axis 6.5 inches. This massive geographic phenomenon shifted Japan as much as 12 feet closer to North America. We will remember that day for hundreds of years. How can such an event be measured or even comprehended?

With tsunami-like impact, a wave of ink has hit Western civilization. No, buildings are not toppling and lives are not being swept away. But with a force of sudden, unexpected, and seismic proportions the tattoo phenomenon is smashing into our lives and culture just as surely as the Pacific Ocean rushed six miles inland, surpassing all human ingenuity and preparedness to mitigate the event. Tattoos are everywhere, and this is bigger than anyone can measure, let alone explain.

Once a disrespected art form that was banished to seedy alleyways, tattoo artists with police records, and storefronts that otherwise couldn't be rented, tattoos are now mainstream and growing. An anchor tattoo on Granddad's forearm, a memory from WWII, has now graduated to full-color arm sleeves and even full-body suits. The movement gained significant momentum in the 1990s as famous people like Johnny Depp, Mike Tyson, and David Beckham sported tattoos. Now even runway models, grandmas, and Baptist preachers display their art with confidence, sending messages to all who dare to look.

I can't help thinking about Ol' Blue Eyes, who immortalized Cole Porter's tune:

I've got you under my skin,
I've got you deep in the heart of me,
So deep in my heart that you're really a part of me.
I've got you under my skin.

What was he saying about the secrets of the soul?

But it's just a fad, right? Like hula-hoops, bell-bottoms, or (heaven forbid) the 1970s polyester leisure suit. And yes, I wore one for my prom. Decades later when my kids saw the pictures, they thought I was wearing a clown suit! I said, "Yes, I was," then quickly changed the subject!

Fads come and go, and the reactionaries who think the world has gone to hell are tricked again as long skirts replace micro minis, big hair is cut short, and gas-guzzlers yield to eco-friendly electric cars.

Fads come and go. They're a way a generation chooses to speak, be seen, be whimsical, live and play.

But the tattoo phenomenon is not behaving that way. They are not easily or painlessly erased, even by the best technology available. You live with them, and they become part of your very being. They remain forever, even as the skin changes over time. Terry, the waitress in the diner, said these parting words to me, "When I die, people will be able to read my story, because my tattoos will go to the grave with me."

Some people ask me this reasonable and obvious question, "Al, why this topic? Don't you have more important things to do with your time?" My explanation is that the tattoo culture—the illustrations, their messages, their owners and their lives—has simply captured my heart and my imagination. The research I've conducted has induced tears and deep discussions, created lifelong friendships, and caused unexpected chaos. There was one time, for example, that I was thrown out of one tattoo parlor only to be embraced with love and brotherhood by its competitor across the street.

As an ordained minister on the loose outside of the traditional brick-and-mortar church where I pastored for 24 years, I'm seeing and tasting what's beyond the walls of the sanctuary, in the wild. Or as some might see it, for the first time in many years I've stepped outside the rarified atmosphere of church life to breathe the same air everyone else does, rich with a kaleidoscope of people and experiences. I went from being in fellowship with 500 churchgoing people, to being in life and fellowship with more than 500 non-churchgoing people. In a way, it's like I'm on spring break. But to my surprise, an epic cultural event has caused me to notice something going on right under my nose. What I see is forcing me to ask what it is and why.

Research

I have frequently found that the soul writes on the skin, the most immediately available medium, to record messages, mark events, send warnings, and call out for empathy. Are there silly, shallow, and thoughtless tattoos? Of course! Just as I can speak silly, thoughtless, and shallow words, people can make senseless decisions about getting tattoos. But most of the people I've encountered, including some whose images I initially read as signs of shallow thoughtlessness, have not only been deliberate about acquiring their tattoo, their messages and meanings have been deeply significant. You can't judge a book by its cover.

My research process has been a journey all its own. Looking under a tattoo requires the patience of an archeologist, the mind of a philosopher, the heart of a passionate caregiver, and the confidence of a scholar, even when the interview seems to be going terribly wrong. I can still feel the breath of the biker who told me to go to hell—and asked if he could help me get there—after I inquired about the meaning of the bleeding skull on his forearm. I took the warning and backed away.

I have also been struck by the natural conversations I've had with people who were willing to talk with me, conversations that seemed to be waiting to happen. It might surprise you that this readiness of people to reveal themselves is not something I was accustomed to. Sure, I'd had my share of confessional moments with people who chose to confide in me, but even though ministers are in the business of listening to the soul cries that leak out of folks, most churchgoers don't want to reveal their truest selves to their pastors. In my experience, most of them work overtime—whether they are conscious of it or not —to impress the pastor so he will think well of them and, not unlike the biker, "stay the hell away!" And so a polite dance between the nondisclosing parishioner and the noninvasive pastor ensues. Me and them pretending life is ordered, and good and well managed, when it clearly is not. Frankly, it was this artificial spiritual minuet that drove me to ask myself if that's all there was to being a pastor.

Talking to people who wear tattoos, while not always an open pathway, has frequently been effortless and filled with breathtakingly candid revelations. This is what I thought I would have experienced in church. Sadly, church folk (and some pastors) wrap themselves in an invisible tattoo that says, "Because I'm a Christian you already know my story. I believe in Him. He believes in me, and I have been transformed into the image and likeness of God. No need to look beneath the surface. End of story." Subtext: *Though I am a sinner saved by grace, I cannot admit that the image of God in me is still broken, wounded, and distorted. If I reveal the truth of who I am—the part of me that is not Godlike, which I cover with a plastic spiritual wrapper to keep you from getting close to the real me—you will judge me, God may even judge me, and I will be lost. So, let's not talk about who I really am.* Some of the tattoo people I've met fled from church relationships just like this. They couldn't pretend to be someone they knew they were not, even though they longed for acceptance, healing, and love. If the price for being a churchgoer was to deny the truth about themselves, they'd rather abandon the spiritual shrink-wrap and find God some other way.

This helped me stretch my mind to learn new disciplines. The first thing I discovered was that setting up appointments "to talk about your tattoo" just doesn't work. After a series of faulty starts I realized that opening up this type of personal, and sometimes spiritual, introspection with complete strangers requires a totally different frame of reference. Like a budding fly fisherman, I'd have to spend a lot of time in the wild places to find what and who I was looking for. I'd have to wade into the currents of people's lives. I'd have to watch my footing so as not to stumble over rocks in the emotional landscape just below the surface. I'd have to delicately yet deftly dance my line across the surface. I'd have to become a student of human behavior and cultivate huge doses of patience, something that doesn't come naturally for most of us.

I learned that casual encounters, standing in line at Starbucks, going to a blues bars, dancing, stopping for a bite to eat at mom-and-pop diners, visiting college campuses, and waiting to cross the street are fertile ground for personal connection. To the untrained eye it might appear that these simple moments birthed miraculous, nearly engraved invitations for questions. Not so. Here's the secret: I've honed a formula of patient, attentive, listening, watching, and caring, and cultivated a respectful presence that sometimes leads people to invite me to join them in peeling away the layers of their tattoos.

For many of my kind (religious, churchgoing folk), a snarky inner voice can be all too ready to make a snap judgment about a tattooed person. But perhaps the tattooed girl who just walked by was laying bare her soul, signaling her story in hope that you might acknowledge what you'd seen. She may not care about your response at all, just that you have one. Maybe she'd sit for a while on a park bench, in a coffee shop, or linger in the grocery aisle waiting to see if you'd simply smile, honoring the fact that she is, like you, a child of God. You might even say, "Hi, I saw your tattoo. That's something," and then wait for the unmistakable even if not loudly demonstrated clue that she'd be willing to talk about them, or not. From there, who knows? Without having a clue about what I might hear, people have revealed their secrets because I saw *them*, not just the neon-like signs blazing on their shoulders and arms, and because they've experienced my genuine respect and empathy.

My research experiences suggest that tattoos seem to speak from the soul about what is stirring in the heart: loss, pain, love, anger, a search for connection. Whether you're getting your first tattoo or a whole sleeve, my hope is that you will discern my respect and my honest interest in learning why people are getting tattoos at such a furious pace.

Sinatra sang, "I've got you under my skin." So just what is under there?

Above: The tattoos of this brilliant young musician and organic gardener give praise to the living world.

Above: Through her tattoo, this woman, the mother of four adopted daughters, shares the story of her escape from a sad childhood

Chapter 2: Living Tombstones

The living owe it to those who no longer can speak to tell their story for them.—Czeslaw Miłosz

Far from the grave of his mother, who was laid to rest in London, this man says that he can now carry her memory wherever he goes.

When I was growing up, the landscape of America's small towns was pretty much the same from one place to the next. Large or small, nearly every town center included a post office, a gas station, a bank, a bar, a grocery, an all-purpose department store, a school, a town hall that housed government offices, a police station, a fire station, a hardware store (which frequently doubled as a mortuary), a church, and a graveyard. The older the church, the more likely there was a cemetery on its grounds. Weather-beaten, moss-covered headstones with humble inscriptions marked the resting places of lives that would be remembered as long as the stones stood. These are sacred grounds where the living and the dead commune.

But when our country experienced a massive cultural shift spurred by unparalleled economic growth following World War II, everything about our lives changed. Today, the hub of activity once found downtown no longer defines the character of a community because downtown no longer exists. In 1970 Joni Mitchell sang, "They paved paradise and put up a parking lot."

Today, suburban Americans so yearn for the charming paradise of their childhoods that more and more planned, gated, and deed-restricted subdivisions replicate a Main Street experience with "community centers" designed to create a neighborly downtown feel. But it's an artificial environment, because the things people once did downtown are now often done at home on a computer or while browsing the web on a smart phone at the local Starbucks. You can buy anything you need or want with free home delivery. Even banking, distance learning, and church are done online.

Strikingly absent from this virtual town center, however, is death. When was the last time you saw mourners pouring out of a church or had to stop as a funeral procession slowly made its way through town to the graveyard? Look around and try to find the local burial ground where you live. For a lot of us, it's not there.

Of course, people are still dying, and we still memorialize our loved ones with religious and spiritual ceremonies. But now that we no longer depend on a geographical center to order our lives, the burial ground can be anywhere—especially if our loved ones' remains are cremated. According the National Funeral Directors Association, half of those who died in 2017 were cremated. That means visiting a graveyard to commune with the departed is becoming a lot less common. Except for those historic and hallowed places like Arlington

National Cemetery, the Gettysburg battlefield, and Boston's famed Granary Cemetery, the periodic visit to the family plot in the local burial ground has vanished from our collective consciousness. Death's inevitable intrusion on our lives has been hidden away, frequently by the design of developers who reflect our distaste for death in the footprints of their planned communities.

In cities or in suburbia we can drive for miles and never see a cemetery. We live free of the humbling reminder *Here are the dead, and in the not-too-distant future you will join their ranks.* No more do we find our minds drifting to a memory at the sight of a particular tombstone or notice that a fresh grave has been dug. "Who died?" we might have asked the general store owner. And even if you wanted to do so, it's enormously inconvenient to place flowers on a grave that is hundreds or thousands of miles from where you live. Now, a low-maintenance bronze plaque can be placed at ground level, where a mower just needs one pass to get the job done.

But as I watch people, listen to their stories, and pay attention to what I see around me, it seems that we have a deep and abiding need to acknowledge our losses, make sense of them, and stay connected to them. I've lost track of the number of pickup trucks I've followed whose rear windows are dedicated to the memory of a dead son, father, or grandfather. I'm sure you've seen more than a few crosses on back-country roads and along the highway, adorned with names and surrounded by garish plastic flowers to mark a life taken in a fatal accident.

Try as we might to suppress its ominous presence in our lives, death will inevitably shatter every one of us. Small town cemeteries may have closed, new town centers may prohibit their presence, modern mobility may have taken us far from our ancestral burial ground, and the ashes of those we loved may have been scattered to the winds, but there's something about death that stains our lives and it cannot be washed away—at least not on this side of the grave.

Just take a moment to review your life. You will invariably recall the first pet that died, the first relative who died, the first time you lost a close friend to death. After you've set this book down you'll move to another room in your home and see a picture of your deceased grandfather, wife, or child. You'll notice a favorite painting of a scene from some time in your past, a place where you or a member of your family once lived, but which is no longer inhabited by the people you knew and loved. When I recently turned on the TV to find a movie for some evening entertainment, I found that nearly every story was framed around the experience of death. No matter how well or how poorly we cope with it none of us has figured out what to do with death.

Here's a telling indication of death's abiding presence: In my research I have discovered that the single-most frequent tattoo theme is a reference to death. In the absence of cemeteries and tombstones, people in our time mark the profound experience of loss by inking themselves in memory of their cherished dead. In place of granite blocks and headstones, more and more people use a tattoo to signal the resting place of the deceased, the heart. By doing so they become living tombstones, memorializing the communion between life and death in their own flesh, and it's with them wherever they go.

The death of a dream

I met Dan at a tattoo convention where thousands had gathered. I was ensconced in my six-by-eight booth with a banner over me emblazoned with "God & Tattoos: Why Is the Soul Writing on the Skin?"

Dan looked like a bodybuilder about to burst out of the muscle shirt that wrapped his body. He gave a quick glance in my direction as he walked down the hall but instantly looked away. I surmised that something he'd seen, perhaps the sign, repelled him. He sped on through the crowd as if to escape. I watched him. Almost as quickly as he'd looked away from me he suddenly stopped and pivoted, looking back in my direction with a strained expression on his face. I continued watching him as other conventioneers passed back and forth. Pausing for a moment, Dan decided to return. Was he lost? Was he looking for someone or something? No, he was resolutely making his way directly back to me. It was evident that something was going on inside him. He looked like a man who needed to say something. I was afraid he might say it with his body—and I didn't think I'd fare very well if he did.

He stopped directly in front of me but looked through me at the banner. And then, without a word he reached back and stripped off his shirt to reveal an impressive mass of rippling muscle that was tattooed front and back. As he turned to show me his back I saw graceful images of a young and beautiful woman, behind which loomed a haunting image of the grim reaper. And then came the story. Sensing I had been invited to step reverently onto holy ground, I listened with rapt and deeply respectful attention.

They had just been married. They were on their honeymoon. They were cycling across country on their Harleys. Then Dan watched in horror as a truck made a sudden wrong move and collided with his wife's bike. She careened off the side of the truck and flew into a ditch, broken, twisted, and bent. The love of his life was instantly devoured in the ugliness of death. From that moment Dan could find nothing to salve his passionate heartache. He threw himself almost addictively into body building. As he spoke, I felt his wound, raw and present as if the accident had just happened, as if it was the only thing that had ever happened in his life. That's how life-defining death can be.

Eventually Dan decided to mark this transformative moment by etching it on his body. Think of the hours he sat in the tattoo studio reliving the horror of the death of his dream. Think of the hours of physical pain he endured to mark the memory of his beloved wife. His back was completely covered, neck to waist and should to shoulder, with his soul's most significant experience, the love and death of his wife. Dan was compelled to live and feel and process this story, which he carries on the inside, by wearing it on the outside, telling everyone what has become the defining experience of his life.

We treasure life instinctively. Our existence is so incredibly precious. And because relationship is one of the most defining characteristics of what it means to be alive, we cannot easily cover the gaping wound that rips through our soul when someone close to us dies. The death of a spouse or a child are among the most intense losses we face. We endure many other "deaths" in life, too—deaths of dreams, lost opportunities, broken relationships, the discovery and admission of our imperfection, childhood, our parents, unfulfilled and self-sabotaged ambitions, love. These experiences cut to the quick, and there is no escaping the pain, even if for a while the shock of the loss numbs us. In essence, the deaths we suffer literally tattoo our soul whether their avatars ever appear on our skin or not.

Let me say it again: We do not know life without death.

Bearing witness

It can be credibly argued that everyone longs to be at home, where the sights, scents, sounds, tastes, and people fill our souls and express who we are and how we feel. Though we shudder to think it, our most profoundly disturbing experiences are also part of "home." Although it may seem counterintuitive, we carry both death and life within us. It is inescapable. They are equal parts of us. They furnish our home.

The soul demands that we pay homage to the arduous journey that has brought us to where we are, including our slogs through the valley of the shadow of death. Perhaps that's why Halloween is more popular than ever in American culture. Costumes and candy temporarily tame our most feared enemy. Perhaps that's why horror movies are one of the most enduring Hollywood genres. Perhaps that is why people have become living tombstones. Not just because we are tortured souls—but because the soul needs to tell its truth. It needs to tell what it knows, and it knows the anguish inflicted by death. Maybe those who wear the signs of death on their skin are more bravely honest about life than the rest of us.

I'm coming to believe that in polite society we try so hard to hold down the volcanic power of death because we fear it will blow up our lives. And so most of us have worked overtime to scrub our lives of its every trace and blemish. As important to primitive man as tending the community fire, we hold down the lid on life beneath which death thunders its threats.

In March 2015, thirteen manhole covers were blown skyward in the streets of Greenpoint, Brooklyn. Salt mixed with melting snow exposed electrical wires that ignited built-up methane in the city's sewers. A live newscast showed a 250-pound manhole cover shoot more than 100 feet into the air, as people yelled and ran for cover. One fireman was injured and almost killed.

What are we seeing in tattoos that takes account of death? We're seeing that it is an explosive force to be reckoned with. The image might be the grim reaper, or a skull; it might be the name of a relative or friend with their birth and death dates. Sometimes it's angels. I've even seen actual tombstones illustrated on the skin in breathtaking detail. The death tattoo takes different forms, but it is a theme that occurs repeatedly. I believe there's a kind of built-up pressure inside us that comes from the denial of death. So, even if our culture is working overtime to free us from its ugly, wrenching effects, people find ways to commune with those they loved, just as surely as we used to do when we'd visit the cemetery to sit or kneel in silence, utter a prayer, talk to the person in the ground, or simply remember and savor what it used to be like to be with them, and meditate on what it is like now that they are with us in such a very different way. To live is to experience life's fragility—its vulnerability. Perhaps those who mark their bodies with the signs of death are writing the true stories of their lives, complete with all its messy inconsistencies.

Regardless of religious doctrine, we treasure life on a scale so significant that it can hardly be put into words, especially the lives of those with whom we have experienced the closet and most intimate encounters. No matter how we do it, we find ways to preserve and even cultivate the significance of the relationships that we have known. Our need to claim their presence in our lives is a fundamental character of human experience. Whether or not there is a cemetery down the street where my father is buried, there is an internal pressure in me that seeks to tell the world it matters to me that he lived and died, that we were connected, and that we *are* connected. Here's the proof.

Portable graveyard

I was on Assateague Island in Maryland, just below Ocean City. About 10 times a year I drive my truck onto the beach and set up camp. It's glorious even in the rain, snow, or wind. My chocolate Lab makes these pilgrimages with me because he lives for the ball to be thrown down the sand or into the waves. As usual, I stopped at the dollar store to get him some canned food and at Royal Farms gas station for the family-size fried chicken for me. I made coffee in my favorite mug—crafted by my potter wife Deb—coaxed a fire from wood washed up by the tide, and sat back to light a Rothschild 6×50-gauge cigar.

I noticed a hiker making his way up the beach toward the walk-in campsites. His backpack was incredibly wide and stuck out a foot above his head. He looked to be forty-ish and in good shape. His stride had a kind of leave-me-the-hell-alone vibe. Unfortunately for him, human contact at this point was all but unavoidable. He had to walk between me and the waves hitting the shore.

Still, it surprised me when he glanced over and said, "Cool truck, dude."

Always open to the adventure of an unexpected conversation I shot back, "Thanks. Need a break? Want a coffee?"

"Yes!"

I admit, my motives weren't pure because I'd seen his tattoos. They were loud and just waiting to be aired out. I grabbed an extra chair and handed him the coffee. Other than learning his name was Pete, we sat in man-silence for about 20 minutes sipping our hot java.

I calculated that enough time had passed to make another invitation. "I like your tattoos."

"Yeah, they've become my story."

"Looks like you have spent a lot of time, money, and thinking on them. Mind if I ask some questions?"

I rationalized that my truck, coffee, and the offer of one of my precious cigars bought me the right to ask what might have otherwise been invasive questions. Nothing ventured, nothing gained!

He started at his left shoulder. The first tattoo, up top, was a bicycle, fishing pole, and two little-boy arms wrestling, all in one picture. Pete was in fourth grade when his buddy and partner-in-crime Tommy died. He fell off a tractor and was killed on the family farm in North Carolina.

"Why did you put it there?" I asked.

"Oh, 'cuz I'm left-handed. And I found out in my teens that there had been a funeral for Tommy that my parents didn't tell me about at the time. So I missed it, probably for the best. I wonder sometimes if he would have joined the military, like me."

Below the Tommy tattoo was Pete's military unit. He was a tank man. Below the tank was Mother Mary with beads. "What's that mean?" I asked.

"My mom, she died of breast cancer when I was in the military. They sent me home, but she was dead before I got there. Some say the Virgin Mary kept me alive in the military. That's what my mom would have said. I'm not religious but my mom was. Maybe I'll get there one day."

"What does the deck of cards mean, Pete?"

He sighed, "My old man, he smoked and drank himself to death after my mom died. He loved playing Black Jack. That was his nickname—Black Jack."

There were many more questions, and many tattoos to explore, just on his arms! Our cigars were half gone—and so was Pete. "Well friend, I gotta go," he said. "Thanks for the coffee and smoke. What do you do?"

"I'm a minister."

"Really? They smoke cigars?"

"Some do."

"Say a prayer for me," Pete said, as he lifted his military pack onto his broad shoulders. He walked away like a soldier on a mission.

Pete doesn't have to visit cemeteries and put flowers on the gravesites for Tommy, Dad, and Mom. He takes their tombstones with him, all the time. As long as he lives and keeps that arm, his memories will live too. They may be dead, but the people memorialized on Pete's body walk with him, sleep with him, dream with him, rejoice and suffer with him everywhere he goes.

The way we grieve for our dead is something to ponder. We get the shocking news of the death of someone who is special to us. That trauma is compounded if the death was violent or completely unexpected. Like the lightening that rips apart the sky in a storm, our lives are torn by death. We go to the funeral, or not. And then, like the thunder clouds that pass, our life goes on, but not without change. Our hearts are rent by death. In fact, psychologists, funeral directors, ER staff, and clergy all attest to the nearly universal reaction of the next of kin when a death is reported. "Where is he?" "I have to see her!" No matter how much capacity we have for the conceptual and philosophic, when it comes to death we have a primal, instinctive need to account for the body.

Someone somewhere came up with the idea of writing the memory of the dead on their skin. Did you know some tattoos are created with the ashes of the deceased? Could there be any more tangible expression of the soul's need to account for the lives of those who have touched it? Because we are mobile people no longer fixed to a particular piece of ground, cemeteries and headstones are no longer accessible to us as they once were. But we still need to know where the dead are, especially those whose lives have most intimately intersected with ours, those whose flesh and blood and DNA we share. If they are tattooed on us, we know right where they are. They live on us, in us, and with us.

In Western culture, contemporary expressions of grief are rushed, with scheduled funerals and graveside arrangements. Not so with tattoos. They take time and pain to create; they move at the rate of our ability to process the meaning of our loss. They sleep with us, meet us 10 years later, look at us from the mirror, release and capture emotions that come and go, while the tattoo remains, faithful to its purpose— carrying the heart's hurt on the soul's shroud, our skin.

Will Pete still think about Tommy when he's 64? What does 55 years of remembering a death feel like when it's written on your left shoulder and you see it every time you get out of the shower? What's more, the person who has become the tombstone of their dearly departed seems to ask others to see and account for their loss. The startling illustrations that assault us in the grocery store, at Starbucks, and as we reach to shake hands are like book covers and dust jackets of deeply poignant stories. People who wear tattoos of death want not only to remember their loss, they want to be encountered and experienced as people whose multidimensional lives are known and accounted for, too.

In my research journey there have been many people I've interviewed, or tried to, who would give a quick, trite answer when I asked about their death tattoos. "Oh, I just liked the picture," or "It makes me feel good," they would say as they moved away. But others like Pete went into detail and relived their stories. So, I'm left to wonder, is it fair, is it reasonable to ask someone the meaning of their tattoos when its likely we'll hear a story of pain? At the same time, I wonder, are those who carry these signs of death prepared to spend the kind of emotional and psychic energy required to expose the stories of their lives? They write on themselves and pass by our curious eyes.

Everyone has a story. Almost no one I've risked talking to has ignored me, even if they wouldn't tell it, or did so haltingly. Their tattoo stared at me, like a trail of bread crumbs coaxing me along. I'm coming to see that a lot of the people who wear tattoos want to be known—to themselves mostly—and sometimes by others, too.

Missing children

I met Janice at the Ka'Tiki blues bar—a classic "down-at-heel" dive in Treasure Island, Florida—while attending a conference for pastors. (Trust me, there was no connection between the conference and the blues bar, except me.) I could see the Gulf of Mexico from my barstool. It was a Monday night. The band was sort of drunk, but it seemed to be a perfect match for the 60 or so patrons, all of whom seemed to know each other. Everyone's clothes were wrinkled as though they had slept in them for days. The band played one of my Muddy Waters favorites, "I Can't Be Satisfied."

Well I know my little old baby
She gonna jump and shout.

That old train be late man, Lord
And I come walking out.
I be troubled, I be all worried in mind,
Well honey ain't no way in the world could we be satisfied
And I just can't keep from crying.

A lone lady—she looked like a college professor on spring break—
went out and danced in the middle of the floor all by herself. She took
off the light sweater she was wearing, and I could see small, delicate
tattoos adorning her back, and another peeking out from her tank top.
She had that look of a properly ordered society woman who was
dancing like nobody else was watching. At least she didn't seem to
care. The song ended, most of the patrons clapped, and she came and
sat down near me.

"I'm glad someone here dances," I said.

Staring nowhere in particular she replied, "Anyone can dance,"

"I like your tattoos," I went on. She just looked at me. So, I tried
another tack. I told her, "My wife and I like swing dancing. We go out
to dance regularly. Would you like to dance?"

"Well, yes, but I usually get paid."

"Get paid?" I choked.

"Yeah," she said, matter-of-factly.

Not sure what to do with that I pressed on. "I'd like to know what
your tattoos mean. I'm doing some research."

We took the few steps onto the dance floor. I guess my hesitation
was evident. "It's just dancing, not a real estate deal," she said.

She wasn't used to dancing East Coast swing, but she followed
very well and laughed. The song ended, and we sat down.

"So, I have to pay up, huh?" I asked.

"Well, that was the deal," she said playfully. Smiling she reached
down and pulled up the bottom of her shirt exposing the tattoo on the
left side of her rib cage. It was a poem, written in script. I asked if I
could write it down.

"Sure," she said.

We drew some odd stares from people as I copied the words into a
notebook.

There is too much pain. So write ... write for me of happy, of make-
believe, of heaven and eternity, of no pain or misery, of no abuse
or fatality, of no tears or cruelty, no more death for you, no more
death for me, can't you see?

Later I discovered the title for this moving piece: "Too Much Sadness for Me," by Eileen Manassian Ghali.

"What does it mean?" I asked my new friend Janice.

"Do I get another dance?" she asked. I agreed.

As we danced, Janice told me her story.

"I married a man from Pakistan 15 years ago. We met in college. My dad didn't approve, but we were in love. We held a wedding and some our friends came, but neither set of parents attended. We had two kids. I taught advanced math at a local college, and he was an engineer. Then, one day I came home. There was a note on the table. I knew it wasn't going to be good, because we had been fighting for a long time. He took the kids to Pakistan and now considered me to be dead."

What I felt in what she said made my eyes mist. "I am so sorry."

"That was four years ago, I haven't seen my kids for four years."

"How could that be?"

"It's all tied up in the courts—his family has a lot of money, and overseas lawsuits take forever. The poem seemed to say what I needed to hear; it's near my heart like my kids. I know I will see them one day, at least when they are 18 and can make their own decisions. Right?"

A hoppy swing song came on, and I danced again—but this time it was with a woman who was dead to her husband and hadn't seen her two kids in four years. The music was fast, but my feet just wouldn't kick into happy mode, though we lasted till the end of the song.

"Thanks," she said, shaking my hand, and walked away.

As I stood there thinking about her tattoo I could feel my researcher's façade fall away. My curiosity had led me into the most private painful loss of Janice's life. The shock of what I'd heard triggered my imagination. What if I was separated from my kids for four years, when they were six and nine years old?

Janice was no doubt out of money for the lawsuit, with however many years to go. Her dancing alone, like no one was watching, made sense to me; perhaps she was exorcising her demons and pain. I felt bad for being silly and trivial about payment for the dance, dragging her through the death of her marriage and loss of her kids. She responded to her pain by writing a poem on the skin near her heart. Life had stolen away her dearest treasures, but her tattoo signaled her hope.

This was not an easy encounter. Well, the encounter was all right, but its effect on me wasn't. After all, I'm not just a researcher. I'm a person subject to the same kinds of inexplicable and frequently unavoidable life traumas that I've heard from hundreds, now probably thousands of people. A few times I've thought that if I ever see her again—though I know I won't, since like me she was another out-of-town tourist—I would say, "Janice, I am so sorry for the tragedy, and I am so sorry that my childish game exposed the greatest wound in your life. I will pray for you, your children, and a reunion that only God can make happen." I wanted to write her a letter, but maybe that tattoo was the best prayer I could pray, and so I do when I think of this family split apart.

Janice's tattoo is a mother's epitaph to the loss of her children. Maybe one day, maybe in this life, she'll take them in her arms again. But for now, she wears her heart's hurt on the surface of her skin because she cannot let go of those it speaks of. Why should she?

Sudden infant death syndrome

Carmen was a forty-something tattoo artist I met in the Boston area. She was kind and warm to me as I walked in, perhaps assuming I was about to be a paying customer. I am pretty sure she saw right through me as I examined the room, trying to be so cool, pretending to be a veteran of countless tattoo parlors, like I knew exactly what I was doing. Business was slow, and I thought she'd be willing to put up with my research questions. But I sensed that I was *this close* to a brash order to leave if I didn't demonstrate respect by acknowledging the value of her time and expertise. Finally, I told her about my research and asked for her help; then we were interrupted by a real customer who walked in.

Carmen asked, "If I answer your questions are you going to get a tattoo today?" I stalled a few seconds and then choked out, "Um, no!" That created a little humorous tension and tacit permission to keep up with my professional inquiry.

"So, go ahead, ask away!" she said.

"What's that tattoo?" I asked pointing to a picture over her heart.

"It's about my son."

"Your son?"

She paused. From previous experience intentionally asking questions a lot of folks might not dare to, I was fairly certain that

Carmen knew she had just moved into the "should-I-bare-my-soul to-some-stranger-with-a-bad-haircut?" zone

While she pondered whether to keep going I asked, "Why your son?"

She continued her pregnant pause. I wasn't sure which way it would go. Would she give me enough to get rid of me, or open the door that might lead to a broken heart? I waited.

"My son died of SIDS, sudden infant death syndrome, 20 years ago."

"I'm so sorry Carmen. So, so sorry."

"Yeah, this tattoo reminds me of him."

Never one to end an encounter before it needs to, I pressed on as delicately and respectfully as I could, "So, can I read your tattoo out loud?"

"I got nothing better to do," she said.

There are often two levels of potentially awkward intimacy when you ask people about their tattoos. The first is asking the question about an image or inscription that has unseen nerve endings wired directly to the heart. The second is having to strain my feeble eyes to study a portion of someone's body in a way perhaps only a coroner does, only in these cases the body being studied is very much alive. These moments are delicate. The request to see and the invitation to show are among the most sacred invitations to connect I have ever experienced.

If you could see my eyes now
You will read all the untold words.
If only you could see through them
You will understand that for me you are the world.
If only you can feel how fast my heart beats
You will know that you are the one who makes me feel complete.
Mommy

Carmen didn't cry, but I did. "I'm sorry," I said.

"It's okay. Sweet that you think he was something special."

"What was his name, Carmen?"

"Joey, named after his dad. We aren't together anymore. After Joey died so did our marriage. All the energy just ... left."

"I'm so sorry, friend," I said.

In that moment, for some crazy reason, my mind snapped back to a funeral I did for a family five years earlier. On the day he was born they held their baby boy with all the boundless joy new parents feel. But a

47

few weeks later, their joy turned into excruciating pain as they clung to his lifeless body. I remember that family's tears, their hugs, their blank, nonblinking eyes, and the deafening silence as I read the 23rd Psalm. I've seen these very words tattooed on living skin. *"Yea, though I walk through the valley of the shadow of death, I will fear no evil."* (Psalm 23:4)

I will always remember Joey's mom and her poem about their deep connection. Having seen her wound I often ask God to bless her in the midst of her suffering. Is this why there are tombstones, so that the memory lives on? Is this why you wear your heart on your sleeve, so we will see who you really are, what you really care about, and seeing, our hearts will touch each other?

Right: This man says that throughout his life, he lost people closest to him, and that his tattoo reminds him that death is a part of life.

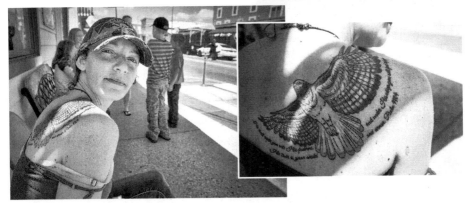

Above: This mother of two boys and organic gardening instructor tells the story of how, after her father died, a red tailed hawk, sent by God, came to her, and since then, those hawks allow her to touch them. Her tattoo is a memorial to her father and a celebration of the bird that carried his spirit.

Below & right: This man uses his body to honor the memories of his beloved mother and dog and express his love of the sea.

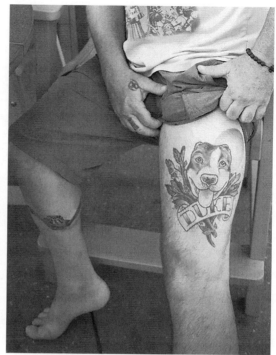

Above: The tattoo that covers his heart is dedicated to the young son he lost.

Chapter Three: Poetry in Motion

Poetry is when an emotion has found its thought, and the thought has found words.
—Robert Frost

This stunning painter encourages people to use tattoos as an art form—a way to have fun, explore, and get out of their boxes.

How many times can you reinvent the hamburger? Many times, it turns out. Pittsburgh's Burger Joint is one of those cool restaurants that creatively customize the experience of enjoying the classic American burger. The one-pounder I had was mouth-watering and filled me up until Lent.

The waitress, Tina was in her mid-thirties, pretty, with a plucky attitude. I saw a tattoo draped over her shoulder. The print was too small for me to read, and I couldn't see it all. When you study tattoos without the wearer's knowledge you have to strain to catch glimpses of what's there, because the body is constantly in motion. Even the subtlest movement challenges my old eyes.

What I did see told me she had spent a lot of time thinking before anyone was given permission to write on her skin. Her beauty was natural, and the tattoo needed to compliment, not distract from, her glow.

"I like your tattoo," shifting my gaze from her face to her shoulder.

She cast her eyes over to it and said, "Yeah, it's me and the moon." Without skipping a beat she asked, "Like your burger?"

"Yes, and could you roll me to my car please?" We both laughed.

I waited to see what might come next, and the pause paid off.

"I got divorced this year and so it's just me and my five-year-old daughter. We're making it, but it's been hard, and dark. But even when its dark, sometimes the moon keeps you company. Right?"

People constantly ask for my agreement as if they need me to validate their point of view. When they do, just beneath the spoken word I hear, *I feel a little awkward here, telling you this stuff. And I'm kind of embarrassed about it. I mean, I don't say this to just everyone. So could you sort of let me know that I'm not making a fool of myself by exposing what I think and feel?* Yes, I hear all of that in a single word. Most of the time I don't say anything. I just listen and pay attention with an open heart and mind to see what comes next. And it did.

"My daughter has nightmares about daddy never coming back again."

I waited again, not moving a muscle, poised so I wouldn't miss the appearance of what it might be that Tina wanted to show me. She must have known that my pause was assurance that she was safe letting her heart speak, because that's what she did.

"Loneliness comes in the middle of the night sometimes, when I can't sleep. I found that the moon became a reminder that there is hope, and while some things change, others stay the same. The moon and me, we became good friends."

"Bless you friend," I said.

Reading this encounter between me and the tattooed waitress you might be clamoring to know, "But why didn't you say something more? Why didn't you affirm her?" Well, I did. I affirmed her by listening, by being respectfully inquisitive, by noticing the invitation written on her shoulder that asked, maybe even begged, to be read. And by positioning my heart and mind toward her, not getting caught up in my own internal dialogue. I was just there.

As I stood up to leave, she hugged me, and then looked into my eyes for a moment, as though she was happy to be understood. I smiled and nodded.

Tina didn't just tell me something she might not tell others. It was the way she told me. Her tattoo was pretty, it was graceful. The words she used were more than a factual explanation of the image on her shoulder. She was speaking to me in a poem. Not in rhyming words, but in a musical, metaphorical depiction of something greater than either the tattoo or her words.

In the language of poetry, carefully arranged words can penetrate the soul and create images in our minds. Sometimes even a snarky and judgmental observer can be captured by the poetry in the words, color, messages, art, placement, or even the movement of the wearer of the tattoo. Poems invite us into the realm of imagination. Story, fact, feeling, fantasy, exaggeration, soundless music, and silence can all converge in line and verse.

Poets have always been both storytellers and philosophers. I've also found that to be true of many who wear tattoos. Poems can say what needs to be said in ways that a Facebook post or cell phone video never could. Small groups of words, phrases, and even sentences—the blueprints of poetry—can live quite well as a tattoo on the canvas of our skin. Nearly every encounter I've had with people who wear tattoos has had a poetic flow about it. People like Tina speak in poetry and, I am learning, process their life experience as a poem—a flowing stream of events, people, and intuition that travel together, sometimes synthesized, sometimes just as individual elements. For more than a few of the folks I've met, their tattoos seem to have released their hearts, as if their newly inked story was the hinge that allowed them to open a door constructed out of fear and pain, behind which lay a long-hidden reservoir of meaning, insight, and beauty.

Poems can be dangerous because they often trigger emotions we thought were safely tamed, medicated, and forgotten. When I hear familiar lyrics from the 1970s, my whole being—my nervous system, muscles, gut, mind, and my heart—can be transported in a nanosecond back to the time when I was a carefree teen, trying to get *just one girl* to notice me. In the same way, the poetic lyrics of tattoos can transport their owners to another place, another dimension, and a reality other than the one in front of us.

Poems can lower our blood pressure, stop hate for just a moment, or imagine a love that is always speaking. Tattoos are amazing conduits for the poetry of the soul. Sometimes I've found it difficult to separate the elements of an experience with a person who's revealed him- or herself to me. I can't, nor is there a need to, draw a line between the tattoo image, the words spoken, and the story I hear. And that's where the poetry of a person's life, symbolized in their tattoo, might be more dangerous to an observer than for the person who has already stepped into the depth and breadth of their own experience.

Why? Because I am often not primed and ready to go where someone else's experience has already taken them. Maybe that's why some of us stop in our tracks when we see a tattooed person. Like walking in on someone using the bathroom, we're taken aback by the exposure of what we are sure we should not have seen. Some of us are threatened or even repulsed by the transparent honesty of the person wearing their tattoo, even if we don't know what is being said. And we're not sure we want to know.

Left behind

Late one night, after leaving my local blues bar, I made a ritual stop at the nearby 7-Eleven in search of junk food. As I looked up and noticed the security cameras, I wondered what the team analyzing tonight's video would determine about me. As I aimlessly paced the aisles was I telegraphing "There's not a damn thing worth eating here?" Or would they conclude, "Yep, there's a shoplifter all right," or "Give me a break, it's another one of those guys who stands and reads the newspaper but never buys one."

Laughing at myself as I imagined these scenarios, I queued up to buy my munchies. The young man in line ahead of me grabbed my attention. His sunburned arms had striking tattoos, and there was a good bit of writing. I nonchalantly asked, "Son, after I pay could I ask you about your tattoos? It looks like your trying to say something."

"Sure man, I've got a few minutes." I sensed he might have been suspicious, but he was agreeable.

We walked out onto the concrete where it looked like many coffees had been spilled that day.

"So, what does this one say?" I asked, pointing to his arm. He quoted it verbatim without looking at it. I wrote furiously on my donut bag.

I want you to love me
Just one more day
And let me feel those nice
Feelings once again
Let me forget that you already went away
Cause that will make me go insane.
Let me love you one more day
To give you more love
That may make you stay
Come back to my life, once again appear.

Stay in my heart, come near and remove this fear
Let us fall in love once more
And from this dream don't make me awake.
Don't say goodbye, don't close the door, for heaven's sake.

"Wow, I didn't see all of that there," I said, and then went quiet, waiting to see if I'd get the backstory.

He pulled up his muscle shirt and showed the rest of the poem written from the top to the bottom of his of his ribcage. Yup, it was all there.

"She left me for a rich college boy," he said. "He had a nice car, rich dad, and took her on a vacation with his family. She didn't tell me about the trip till she came back and broke up with me."

"I'm sorry man, really sorry."

"Yeah, I wanted to forget her, and then—bam. I wrote this whole damn poem on me."

He had grease under his nails as though he'd just come from work at a garage. And he had a wounded love buried under his tattooed skin as though he'd just experienced a broken relationship that defied every kind of repair.

56

Taking it in

Have you noticed how fine art has become more mobile? I've seen some of the very same exhibits in many of the cities I've visited over the past ten years. The city council will tell you they sponsor these because it's good for the citizenry. Art's truth inspires. It lowers the crime rate, gives people another reason to gather and experience a sense of community.

Art in public spaces seems to bring out the goodness in people. An intangible quality of inspiration seems to envelope them, making them happier, more courteous and considerate, creating a sense of curiosity, and elevating the experience of being alive. I can't measure this, but I feel it, I see it, I sense it in others. I'll bet you have too.

Another kind of traveling art has moved into our public spaces—tattoos. People themselves have become public exhibits. They are inches away from us on the elevator, walking past us on the way to work, adorning the frames of wafer-thin runway models, and decorating the arms, necks, and even heads of contemporary nondenominational millennial preachers.

Tattoos are mobile works of art that live and move in the cryptic poetry of a human being's existence. A quick flash of verse catches our eye before its owner disappears, leaving us with questions that hang like billowing clouds in the sky. What to make of it is, as they say, up to the one who beholds it. Only the blind and callous dismiss today's sunset as merely one of thousands. Those who are attentive know this day's last rays of light are not those of yesterday or tomorrow. Whether you see and can confidently claim to fully comprehend the tattoo is not the point. It is whether you can allow the unexpected and often unintelligible to reveal itself to you by simply being attentive to what is there.

Ever heard of a poetry slam? It's a gathering of people who listen as each one in turn speaks their experience, their truth, their perception in verse. The spoken word, their vehicle of self-expression, stirs a powerful response that rolls like thunder through the audience. It's every bit as powerful as the spirit-swelling music that pours out of Louisville's Fifth Street Baptist Church on a Sunday morning. It's a multidimensional experience of individual declaration that fires the imaginations of those who hear and respond.

Think of a slowly materializing rain—one drop at a time, each distinct, but each building one upon the other until soon millions of drops collide on the roof above your head, sounding like a symphony. We live in a poetry slam every day, made up of sights, sounds, and our responses to them. More and more, tattoos are like fibers being woven into the many-colored coat of our lives. These fibers speak, they sing, they dance, they evoke feelings, sensations, and awareness just as surely as the aroma of mom's cooking, the sound of summer's cicadas, and a frosty blast of winter wind on your face. The art of life is captured in the images and etchings of tattoos, moving all around us. Do you see it? Can you hear the poem of life being written in our time and space?

I have watched visitors to Spain's National Gallery, one of the world's leading art museums, rush past works created by none other than Pablo Picasso—probably the most famous artist of the twentieth century—as if they weren't even there. One time, as a group of tourists passed an iconic Rembrandt painting, I heard one of the visitors say to his companions, "You know, they're all the same. You've seen one, you've seen them all." Really? You don't have to be in a world-famous gallery to make this mistake–though it is much more noticeable there. Sometimes we unconsciously rush past the unique art on display all around us. Perhaps we see it but don't like it, or we assume it is all the same. Still, the motion and movement of the tattoo adorns our public space with its art, its poetry. Have you missed it? Go and look again.

Poems are full of hidden meaning and nuance. Some poets only write for themselves, others have huge audiences and standing ovations. Poetry can elicit emotion from a calloused heart, make a grown man cry, reopen old wounds, or recall cherished memories. Poems cause us to slow down, exhale, and imagine other worlds, forgotten history, and ancient civilizations. Poets challenge us to think and feel more deeply. I encourage you to take another look, or see for the first time. Tattoos are poetry, to be read, to be heard. They're not just for their creators. They're for you too.

Many, many years of stories cover this man's body and reveal his sense of humor.

Right: This man used his name to create his tattoo design.

Chapter 4: Weaponize Me

A weapon is a device for making your enemy change his mind. — Lois McMaster Bujold

Hailing from Chicago, this man says he'd always been fascinated by gangsters.

One of the most rough-and-tumble characters in American history was Theodore Roosevelt, the 26th president. TR, as he was called, was a rare combination of statesman, politician, philosopher, and warrior. He was the quintessential man of action. TR made an indelible mark on the country—and the world for that matter—with exploits that illustrated his "cocked, locked, and ready" disposition.

In 1897, while serving as assistant secretary of the navy, Roosevelt used his influence to build support for US military intervention in Cuba's revolt against Spain. Harkening back to the first president of the United States, he quoted George Washington: "To be prepared for war is the most effectual means of protecting the peace." When the USS *Maine* mysteriously blew up in Havana harbor on February 15, 1898, killing 267 servicemen, the country rallied to Roosevelt's message. Barely a month later America declared war on Spain.

TR did two things. First, he ordered the Pacific Fleet under Admiral George Dewey to capture the Philippines, then under Spanish control. And then, in an action that most of his contemporaries judged proof of his unstable temper, he quit the office of the navy to join the fight! Obtaining a commission as lieutenant colonel, Roosevelt created and led the first US Volunteer Cavalry Regiment, the Rough Riders.

With the debut of Thomas Edison's moving pictures, Americans saw Teddy and his swaggering band of cowboys and former military men leave Tampa, Florida, for Santiago, Cuba. His famous assaults on Kettle and San Juan Hills catapulted Roosevelt into the limelight, bringing him meteoric fame and popularity. He was elected governor of New York in 1899, and shortly afterward became vice president under William McKinley. Then, almost as quickly, TR was elevated to the presidency in September 1901 when the 25th president was assassinated only six months into his second term.

TR was wildly popular as a take-charge leader. He not only finished the unexpired term of his predecessor, but handily won a second term on his own merit. Throughout his tenure as the nation's chief executive, TR regularly hunted, rowed, and even boxed. On one occasion he was blinded in one eye during a bout with a young naval officer. He significantly influenced the development of college football and its regulations. He saw the sport as a way for young men to reenact Civil War battles. He believed in living what he called "the strenuous life," writing, "I have no envy for a man who lives a life of ease."

In a letter dated January 1900, TR penned one of his most quoted lines: "Speak softly and carry a big stick; you will go far." He reiterated that maxim in a speech eight months later at the Minnesota State Fair, just two weeks before he would become president. These words capture his never-resting second sense about the inevitability of a fight. And in the fight was exactly where he wanted to be.

Demonstrating his "big stick" diplomacy as president, in 1907 Roosevelt ordered a battleship group, the Great White Fleet, to circumnavigate the globe, a 43,000-mile journey. Just as when he was assistant secretary of the navy, TR wanted America's might on full display to deter hostile actors. It was an impressive sight: 16 steel-hulled battleships, grouped in two divisions. Roosevelt repurposed the navy to project American power. It became an impressive military force that—well, spoke softly but obviously acted as a big stick.

Theodore Roosevelt, warrior-leader and man of action, carried himself in the world as a "weaponized" man. It was as if he wore the navy's guns as a grand floating tattoo that sent the unmistakable message: "Don't mess me. Don't mess with us. Don't mess with this!"

But why? Could his public life have been a response to the private one? TR was a sickly child who struggled with asthma. But he fought back by becoming an athlete, overcoming what for most in his day was a crippling obstacle. Later in adulthood, his mother and wife died on the very same day. These losses were crushing blows that nearly ended his career in public service. But again, he fought back, though he never again mentioned his wife's name.

The prowess of our 26th president demonstrates the effectiveness of projecting power. Such messages are all around us every day. They say, "Don't mess with me, or else."

I often see that kind of warning in the tattoos worn by people who have very consciously inked themselves with images and symbols designed to warn others to back off—everything from mutilation, alien life-forms, and deviant sexual extremes—haunting images that depict a soul racing to the bottom. The explosion of dark art in our culture has magnified the power and intensity of these messages. Why? Are the people who wear these images threatened by those who might come too close? Are they compensating for a weakness that they are afraid makes them vulnerable? Or are they combative and violent for another reason? Are they engaged in a contest we can't see? I'm not sure. But I think

I've discerned these possibilities at work in some of the people I've interviewed.

Personal security system

I met Jason in Stuart, Florida, at the Terra Fermata Tiki Bar. He was in the back, wearing a black leather vest. No shirt, no hair. He had a pretty girlfriend, perhaps in her forties.

Half of Jason's face was tattooed, like the half-mask of the Phantom of the Opera. Every inch of exposed skin had a design on it—the tops of his hands, his one ear, the top of his head, and of course all along both arms and neck. There were motorcycles and burning skulls, explosions with body parts flying, and many, many snakes.

He caught me staring at him. It was awkward.

"Peace, brother," I greeted him.

I introduced myself, extending my hand. He didn't take it. This is going well, I said to myself.

"I'm researching tattoos. Wondering if I could ask your opinion?"

The girlfriend spoke up. "He can come off as unfriendly sometimes, but there's a real human in there. His name is Jason, mine is Silver. What questions do you have?"

Jason was just sitting there, staring away from me, not talking, as if he didn't want me to be there, as if I might be wise to take a hint. But, I took Silver's invitation as a bit of cover. So, I continued.

"What do your tattoos mean?"

Finally, the silent Jason spoke.

"F**k you, f**k the world, and f**k everyone!" He laughed sarcastically as if to say, "You wanted to know what they mean? You asked, man. That's what they mean!" I think he assumed I'd melt away. A lot of others probably had. Or maybe they weren't as naively inquisitive and read him from a distance and simply stayed away. Not me. I kept on.

"Why?" I asked.

"WHY?" As if to say, "Listen moron—do I have to explain myself to you? Don't you get it?"

He went on. "This is the most f**ked up place: babies die, families can't earn money to be together, disease killed my old man, and my mom is a crazy lady with dementia." Then looking at me with an honestly penetrating gaze, "What planet, may I ask, do you live on, sir?!"

Whoa! This guy was a powder keg with a very short fuse. And for all my exposure to some very wild stuff over the years, for all my inner conviction that I was ready for whatever someone might dish out, this interview was definitely turning on me. But I wasn't going to shrink away. I wanted to know more. What was underneath? What was inside?

"I hear you friend." Thinking that the "babies die" line might have some personal connection, I asked, "Do you have kids?"

"Yeah. But, they don't talk to me."

Moving on. "What is the tattoo on your forearm?" I could have picked any one of dozens of images. But his arm caught my eye.

"Got that in prison. It was for protection."

No surprise. I could easily conjecture he'd had, let us say, an altercation or two over the years. He'd inked himself with a message that would keep people away, like a personal security system that warned intruders they'd pay a heavy price if they got too close.

"Will you get more tattoos?"

"Yup," he answered. "Haven't done my back yet. Me and Silver are gonna tell our story on me."

I've heard and seen this before. People illustrating their life on its wrapper. I'm always intrigued. Is the story illustrated so others won't ask? So they will ask? Or so the storyteller can hold onto the visceral pieces that they have so keenly felt, that remind them of who they are and what happened to them?

The band was getting ready to play. I asked, "Anything else you can tell me?"

Silver spoke again.

"All these bad and dark tattoos don't mean Jason is a bad person, OK?"

There it was again, asking for affirmation, like the waitress's "Right?"

"Sure," I thought, nodding in agreement and smiling.

"Peace, friend," I said, and fist-bumped Jason, who responded to the symbolic end of our conversation.

Unspoken messages

Like my encounter with Silver and Jason, most of my tattoo interviews are unplanned. They always seem to go better, and frankly I glean more from the surprised person's responses. To be sure, like paying attention to a dog's growl, I've learned to be respectful and back off when someone gives me a warning. Most of the time these aren't direct. I listen to what is said well as what is not spoken.

Often a tattoo interview comes to a screeching halt when we get to a place beyond which the person is unwilling to go. They don't say, "I'm not going there." They just stop talking, look away, change the subject, or walk off. And, there have been a few threats that have made it abundantly clear the interview is over.

At times I feel as though my questions are attached to a metal detector, passing back and forth over the skin, seeking a hit. Once emotion or thoughtfulness emerges, I switch interview tools and take out a little shovel to dig at that very place, then hold what I find up to the light. When I do this, sometimes the person I'm interviewing sees it for the first time, or they see it differently than they ever have before. Depending on what I sense about the find, and my host's willingness, I decide whether what has been unearthed is worth exploring further.

I enter every encounter with the assumption that I am or soon will be on the sacred ground of someone's life, the place most protected, most cherished, that holds the most mystery and meaning. The right to be there is granted solely by the person whose territory it is.

I usually see a signal that something is there, just beneath the ink, a rich vein of life experience. There's usually a sign, too. Sometimes it says NO TRESPASSING, but there's always a sign. But even the ones that say STAY AWAY seem to ask to be explored. And that is what I do. Tattoos have taken me to some amazing places.

I get to listen, and see, and probe, and show, and hear some more—but only as long and as deeply as the person whose life I am exploring permits me to be there. I am frankly shocked, humbled, and honored by what people dare to show me.

I've discovered that the inked host is not necessarily aware of the full meaning and purpose of their tattoo. I know, it sounds a bit counterintuitive. You'd think that someone who goes to the trouble of suffering the pain, devoting the time, paying the cost, and enduring the public gawking afterward, would think once, twice, or three times about what they are doing. And to be fair, most do. But there's something about a tattoo, and the person's instinct, the feeling of being compelled to get it, that is beyond their comprehension—at least for a time.

Perhaps there are other folks out there like me who are taking more than a cursory look at the ink on people. But I think they must be very few because most of the people I talk to seem to indicate that hardly anyone has figured out that there just might be a connection between the images etched on their outside with the deep and abiding significance of what those images represent to them that on the inside. Sure, their friends will say, "nice tattoo." But in my travels and conversations, I don't get the sense that my tattoo friends have had a lot of soul-piercing, in-depth conversations about their tattoo. Don't get me wrong: I've been blown away by some of their stories, and even more with some of their insights. What I'm saying is that not a lot of people want to go to the deep places that a tattoo signals are lying beneath the surface, or maybe they don't know how to.

So, when I've asked about someone's tattoo, and stayed with them even after a silence that most cognizant adults would understand was a blazing neon sign flashing "Move on, nothing to see here," I've persisted. And amazingly—not always, but often enough—I've watched as people start to metaphorically undress themselves, layer by layer, to reveal things to themselves that they might not have been aware of before, or they might have not known how to begin to talk about. Like going into a dark cave with a flashlight that is woefully underpowered to illuminate the immense space that is there, it can be daunting for anyone to go spelunking in the caverns of their own lives with only a little light. Who knows what any of us might find there, away from the dimly lit entrance?

When people talk to me it seems that they are processing the meaning of their tattoo out loud. And the more they talk, the more it leads some to a deeper discovery of what the tattoo is all about. Invariably, it's about their life. Sometimes I hear what the tattoo meant when they got it. But often I hear stories that seem to come to life before my very eyes and ears. And from these experiences I've discovered that a tattoo is hardly ever just what it looks like. Its meaning, its depth, its significance to the person who wears it changes over time. The tattoo hasn't changed, but the awareness of its significance has now been released to the person's conscious life. It's like a time capsule etched on the skin that holds not only things from long ago, but also the here and now, and even realms and experiences beyond the current time, much like dreams.

Ever read a good book that years later suddenly appears in your thoughts? You want to go back to it, to see what's there, to relive what you experienced the first time. If you're like me, you've not only relived the first experience of the book, but you've acquired additional layers of insight that take you by surprise because you didn't have that reaction the first time. Or—and this is very eerie—you go back to read a story that you were sure had certain plots and characters and themes only to realize after searching from cover to cover that the story you remembered is not the original story. In fact, you have developed the story into something else based on a whole set of intangibles that have influenced your recollection.

You have rewritten the story because life itself is a never-ending story. This happens over and over again with people who get tattoos. While the image itself doesn't change (although it's impossible not to because it is etched on human, living skin and we all change, every day) the heart and soul, where experiences and messages live, are not static. They know the secrets and realities that were not immediately evident the day the tattoo was applied.

Some tattoos are born in the wake of a long night of drinking; others come after years of careful thinking about how much it would really hurt. Some interviews make me flash back to bedtime with my children when they were little. I would take a book and spin a tale about one of its pictures as they tried to stay awake. Indeed, some hosts were, intentionally or unintentionally, a living, breathing storybook.

But many times, these stories are dark and angry, almost like Tim Burton's *The Corpse Bride or The Nightmare before Christmas*. Darker still, I've seen some tattoos that are like a trailer of the horror flick that their owners live every day. I've heard some tattoo owners say profound things about life, even quoting Plato or his student, Aristotle. But then came those who were dark, with scary tats that seemed to beckon from the bottom of an abyss. In *Batman: The Dark Knight Rises,* Bane says "Ahh, you think darkness is your ally? You merely adopted the dark. I was born in it. Molded by it. I didn't see the light until I was a man." These could be the words of many a person who has told me of their darkness.

There is a curious phenomenon, like my encounter with Jason at the Tiki bar, that can rattle me even if I tell myself I'm not going to let it. The body of a man—or woman—that has been transformed into a lethal weapon by etching every inch of skin with words and images of violence and darkness. To see such a sight is more than overwhelming. It can be shocking. The sight stirs something deep inside me.

If a lot of us dart our eyes away from the intruding tattoo on someone's neck, arm, or shoulder, imagine the power of an entire body covered in threatening images. It strikes me that the people who've turned their entire human canvas into a disclosure of their interior story, sometimes a living nightmare, have positioned themselves like Rodin's famous sculpture, *The Thinker*. They are sitting at the gates of hell, threatening anyone who would dare them to go back in to the dark place. *This is me. I'm here. I'm in this space. I'm not going away. So, leave me the hell alone, or come closer at your own risk. You've been given fair warning.* Would you shudder at the prospect of that kind of encounter? I have, more than once.

Too hot to handle

Cus was standing in line, in all his tattooed glory, outside a seafood restaurant in Ocean City, Maryland. By now you might think I've got radar going when it comes to tattoos. But trust me, this guy was inked so prolifically that what I saw driving by would have caught even a blind man's attention; his dramatic skin art had turned everyone there into a voyeur. And I've got to wonder if that wasn't the point.

I thought, "I gotta see if he will talk to me." I drove around the block and parked my car. By now he was halfway up the line waiting to get inside to place an order. I was unsure about my next move, so I loitered, trying to remain undetected. As I waited, the tattooed man came outside with his food and went around one side of the building. I followed him at a distance, trying not to give the impression that's exactly what I was doing.

Rounding the corner to the covered outdoor picnic area, I saw a whole table of guys that looked just like Cus. Wow! Either I had hit the mother lode for tattoo interviewing or I was surely going to regret the effort. I walked up to the table of and asked if they would help me.

"With what?" the older guy asked.

It seems like the bolder and louder and more numerous the tattoos there are, the surlier the response to my questions. I felt like the clean-cut geeky kid who showed up at the burger stand and asked what the biker guys were doing. This gang was signaling that I wasn't one of them and that I didn't belong there. But, as usual, I wouldn't take the unspoken no as an answer.

"I'm researching tattoos and need help. I'm sort of desperate and would appreciate anything you would tell me."

One guy made a joke about what they should charge me: money or skin. The idea didn't strike me as humorous. Another asked if I was a detective. "Hmmmm, had trouble with the law," I thought to myself. A third said "Go to hell!" Yep, this was shaping up just like I feared it might. But I'd been here, in this no-man's-land between ordinary life and a counterculture group brandishing their tattoos to ward off all outsiders. Would I be allowed in?

One offered, "Tell you what, I'll give you 10 minutes, then you leave, okay?"

"Okay," I decided to take what I was given. "I appreciate your time. Why do you have tattoos?"

"All kinds of reasons!" quipped one, as if I should have known that.

"We don't have time for this," snarled another guy at the same time. My jackpot was beginning to turn into fool's gold. But I've learned not to take first responses as the fullness of what might eventually come. A fair number of people, and these guys were a prime example, want to know if I am really serious or a gawker just pretending to be interested. So, I brushed off these salvos as a test to find out if I could stand my ground. I stood.

One guy who was more accommodating pressed on as if his buddy hadn't said anything. "Life's a bitch, so why not call it what it is?" At that, two others spontaneously gave each other an energetic high-five, post-middle-aged tattooed biceps flapping as they did.

Then came a torrent of first-person testimonials. "I got this one after a car wreck," one man pointed to a tree with a broken trunk.

Another showed me a heart bleeding from a bullet wound. "I got this after my second wife left me."

One guy announced that he'd like to "scare the f**king devil, and I know where he lives!" That started a huge round of banter about who was the real devil in the group. I heard a few names. The guy I'd originally spotted was called Cus. For a moment they forgot I was there.

When the debate about who among them was Beelzebub had finished, someone turned to me and said, "All right, one more question then you leave."

So, I went for it. "What would your mom think of your tattoos?"

Yes, these words came out of my mouth in the presence of roughnecks who could have done serious damage to me in seconds. Months later, when I discovered the Sorry Mom Tattoo parlor in Fredericksburg, Virginia, I remembered this moment. The question took the group to another level.

As if I'd unknowingly flipped a switch, one guy abruptly announced "I'm done." He got up and left in disgust. Suddenly there was a strange and unexpected quiet.

A guy on my left who'd said nothing the whole time, looked up at me, "She wishes I didn't have them, but says she can still see it's me."

A guy in the back behind his buddies chimed in, "My mom is full of hate, who cares?"

The most approachable guy in the bunch spoke again. Pulling up the front of his shirt he said, "You see this tattoo?" Seared over his heart was a rose with the letters M O M and the year she died, 1988.

I'd stumbled once again on this recurring theme: Life is hard. Of course, I know that from my own experience. But there was something jarring about seeing that truth exposed in the words, expressions, emotional pain, and violent body art screaming from this group of men. You can't talk someone else out of their pain, even though a lot of us try to or wish we could. I couldn't deny what was staring me in the face. It was agonizing, like watching a house fire. There was nothing I could do about it, except watch, and ache, and cry inside for their losses and the frustrating helplessness I felt. Why didn't I heed their warning in the first place, and just stayed away?

The power of the emotion they expressed was unmistakable, almost frightening. The depth of their wounds from loss and abandonment was palpable. In fact, in hindsight it's almost as if at the outset I'd been told "The pain of our lives is so severe we can only talk about our tattoos for ten minutes. More than that is beyond our ability to handle. So, get to it buddy. The clock's ticking."

In our brief exchange—which was really 10 minutes times five lives—their tortured stories were on full display. Their struggle with darkness was something they could not fully express. Yet, they were compelled to acknowledge it. How? By wearing it on their skin. Maybe that's the purpose of their body armor—to signal to others, "I'm in such deep, desperate, darkness I can only be with people like me."

It struck me that at some level each man had accepted himself. There was certainly no pretending going on, except for being tough in the face of the demons that haunted their hearts. I was warned right from the get-go. I saw their freakish displays and so did everyone else. I wanted to know what it was all about. I didn't find out all, but I did find out some. Relations had mortally wounded them and now they were trying to survive, despite feeling like the living dead. Still, misery loves company. Everyone needs to feel connected, understood, and known. I couldn't help thinking that they were fortunate to have found each other. Were they so desperate to be found that they had no choice but turn the barrier between their outer and inner lives into a window?

I tried to say thank you the best way I could.

"Guys, you allowed me to interrupt you. Thanks, you helped me. Peace."

Most gave head nods, the nice guy fist-bumped, and I was gone.

Genocide of the soul

In 2008 I returned for a third visit to Rwanda, Africa. The congregation I used to pastor in suburban Virginia had built a church there and put 200 orphans through school. Their parents had been killed in the 1994 genocidal slaughter that stunned the world. Nearly a million people, 20% of Rwanda's population, were executed with machetes. My first visit to the country was in September 1994, immediately after the murderous rampage. Now, 14 years later, piles of bodies were still exposed to the elements, looking like beef jerky stretched over bone.

This time I was asked to lead a pastors' retreat west of Butare in a Catholic monastery. It was an amazing, uplifting experience. I spent time with the subsistence farmers that fanned out beyond the walls of the monastery. Considering what had happened there, it was a surprisingly happy scene of working families and playing children. I was overcome by the sheer joy that poured out of the children who gathered to sing for me. Many spontaneously erupted in jump dancing, a normal ritual for African church services. My heart was jumping too.

After a week in the bush my traveling companions and I returned to the capitol city of Kigali. I stayed in a humble little hotel for a few days. It came with a breakfast of fufu—a cassava- or semolina-based staple food—and some kind of meat. Each morning I would eat with fellow travelers.

But one morning the friendly conversation vanished. A new group had arrived in the night and they weren't the talking kind: UN International Peacekeepers who'd been deployed to Rwanda's massive neighbor to the west, the Democratic Republic of the Congo. There had been long years of fighting between warring militias throughout the region.

The soldiers' eyes stared as if permanently seeing unspeakable events. They moved about clearly reeling from the effects of post-traumatic stress. They ate in sullen silence. When I was able to coax some conversation from a few they were only able to talk for 15 minutes or so before they'd rush off to throw up. In the middle of our limited exchange some simply got up and walked away, shutting the door to their room, right next to mine.

These troops were completely absorbed by the inexplicable horrors they had witnessed. They were in shock. They simply couldn't process what they had seen because it was so expansively dark that it blotted out everything else, including their own lives. Everything had changed, nothing was the same. Every mention of the Congo was like a needle piercing the eye. The peacekeepers could not cope with questions and people who hadn't seen what they'd seen. There was nothing to do but flee for safety, away from the ordinary experiences and exchanges of daily life.

Many of the people I've engaged who wear dark, weaponized tattoos have a strikingly similar demeanor. They flee from my seemingly innocuous questions with the same time-released reaction that characterized my hotel companions in Kigali. Relying instinctively on lower brainstem function, they cowered from the overwhelming power of the violence that had ripped their minds and hearts to shreds. Raw animal survival bypassed higher brain function to simply survive.

When confronted by terrifying threats to our existence, every one of us looks for an escape hatch. For some their escape hatch, their ejection seat, their fail-safe switch is to parade an arsenal of tattoos for anyone and everyone who moves too close to the place of their most feared experience. It's almost as if they draw a sword, hoping that the sound will drive fear into the heart of the listener and warn them to back off. To me, their fear is not of the person who asks about their

74

tattoo. Their fear is what the encounter will provoke within them, which they feel helpless to tame.

It's as if the deepest hurts and wounds and losses are a violent, uncaged lion living inside them. The person knows he is barely able to contain the lion, but he tries anyway—always on guard, always vigilant about what will rouse the beast to maul the heart further. And just as the strength of a person's anger almost always signals the intensity of their hurt, so the louder, more boisterous, offensive, and vulgar the tattoo display that says, "I can get darker, nastier, grittier than you could ever imagine," the more likely that person is to have endured what they consider unspeakable horror and life-threatening, life-consuming pain. They cannot risk what they are sure will be certain annihilation if someone gets too close. So "Read my tattoo. And stand back."

Like the guys at the seafood restaurant, I've come across tattooed folk who have a sense of equal standing with each other, often wearing similar tattoos. They gather in groups and find like company welcome. Despite the differences in the details of each one's life script, many of these people exist in the same stares, stories, and skin. It's a form of brotherhood. Being accepted into a society that shares the same skin art is like being accepted into a family where there is safety, love, and acceptance, as well as a deep, abiding and frequently unspoken knowing.

Don't miss the significance of what happens to the skin when a person submits to the work of the artist. It is torn, colored, burned, and scarred, just like the life within it. The father who was always drunk, the crackhead mom, the bankruptcy that split up the family, or the constant upheaval that never provided safety or rest—these are the real stories of real people everywhere. I suspect that many who wear tattoos decided they couldn't go on without marking themselves. For some reason, putting a sign on the outside of what's on the inside is just something they had to do. It's as if their tattoo is a sign that says, "This is me, this is what I've lived, this is what I suffer and rejoice over. It matters. It matters so damn much I don't ever, ever want to forget."

If you haven't figured it out yet, let me say it plainly—I hunt for people. The ones who send a sign they want to be known on their terms even if their tattoo seems to say "Stay away." The last thing I've ever wanted was to steal anyone's dignity, hurt their feelings, or mock them. In fact I seek precisely the opposite: to accord respect and worth. That's not an easy thing to do with some people. Like a highly sensitive security system, a person's defenses can be so pronounced that no matter what my motive, my approach, or my words, any movement can be seen as a hostile threat.

I can't wave a magic wand to make someone know I'm not a threat. How could I? I don't know what they've lived. Like everybody else, all I see at first is what's on the outside. So moving closer takes some care and a lot of humility. And when I'm not aware of that at the outset most people are pretty adept at putting me in my place, real fast. So I get it. But when there is an opening, when somebody does risk letting me get a little closer, it feels like I've been given one of life's rarest privileges—letting someone show me who they really are. I think everyone wants that. But not everyone believes it's possible to achieve.

See the me I want you to

I was on my way home from teaching at Covenant Seminary in St Louis. I needed a break. Always on the lookout for interesting people and experiences I stopped at a cigar bar on the Ohio River in Louisville, Kentucky. I remember it was cold outside, but the place was small and cozy. There weren't a lot of choices for sitting, so I plopped myself down near a girl and her guy friend.

After some settling-in small talk I learned her name was Laura. "I like your tattoos," I said.

"Thanks."

"Do they have meaning?"

"Yes."

I waited and took a drag on my cigar. As the smoke drifted away I continued, "I'm curious, they're unique."

The word "unique" might have been the key that unlocked that moment.

"They are my tattoos about my life." There was a striking picture of a woman's face on her shoulder. It was strong and confident.

"Is that you?" I asked.

"Yes, it's the inner me. It's about survival, getting through hard times, and never quitting."

"Quitting what," I asked?

A deep breath followed by a sigh told me that what I was about to hear next was likely close to the center of her heart, if not dead on. "Well, my father's in jail. And I put him there."

"I'm so sorry."

"Yeah, I realized the things he was doing to me as a little girl were wrong, but no one ever believed me—including my mother. Finally, I went to a teacher at my school, and she contacted the police. All hell broke loose, and I lost my family. Great deal, right?"

There it was, her truth right out there in broad daylight, and the familiar "right" telling me she hoped I would understand the life-shattering significance of what she'd just told me. I remember exhaling as if to say, "Wow, I'm sorry, Laura." She heard my unspoken reply.

"So the woman's face?" I asked. "What is that?"

The strength and confidence I'd detected in her tattoo began to speak in her words. "She can survive anything and still be pretty. I will survive and keep going. It's a reminder, but I want others to know that too."

There it was, evidence supporting my contention that tattoos reflect secrets of the soul that the wearer wants others to see because they themselves want to be seen. Or maybe the heart wants to be seen and heard—and held.

Listening to this not-so-light conversation between me and Laura, her boyfriend suddenly decided it was time to go. They got up from the cramped space. "God bless you, Laura," I said as she left. She smiled back.

Signs, signs, everywhere signs

Every group has its own language, a shorthand for quickly transmitting an essential message. Smoke signals, trumpet calls, Morse code, notched doorways, and tattoos are used to tell friend, foe, and prey what the message sender wants to say.

Oddly, tattoos are becoming taboo in one of the most-tattooed communities in history—the military. Among the most accepted practices in nearly every human culture throughout history has been the decoration of the warrior's body, demonstrating his purpose, mission, and resolve. But today, the regulations pertaining to tattoos worn by service men and women in the United States military have become more restrictive. Tattoos must be hidden from view when in uniform. But the tattoo's purpose is to be seen, if by no one else than its owner.

Gangs are another community notorious for wearing tattoos. There are gangs who advertise, warn, and find each other by wearing extreme tattoos. The Japanese have practiced this art form for centuries, and it remains a thriving force in their culture. Members of the *yakuza,* a coalition of crime syndicates, often have full-body tattoos. And when I say "full-body" this includes genitalia. These tattoos, called *irezumi*, are hand-poked, with ink inserted under the skin by handmade tools, sometimes sharpened bamboo, other times steel needles. This process is known to be off-the-charts painful, which only adds to the allure and mystery of the yakuza. Only the strongest can withstand the pain of being completely covered in this gang art. Sixty thousand active yakuza are estimated to be in Japan today; together they form the planet's largest organized crime group.

Gangs and their tattoos come in numbers too many to count. The notorious MS-13, tied to drug and human trafficking, is known for grisly, deadly violence. Gang members' body art marks their membership in a specific gang. Some even commemorate the violence and murder in which they've participated. In MS-13, a teardrop can represent either the death of a loved one or an execution. Gang members often get tattoos from each other, sometimes from an approved gang artist, or while serving time in prison.

While some young men fulfill their need for competition, tests of strength, daring, and bravery in gangs, others do so in gaming. Millions of young men all over the world participate in violent, life-and-death video games. Especially popular now are military, murder, and extermination themes. Some of the most popular are Mortal Kombat, Eternal Darkness, Medal of Honor: Frontline, Resident Evil 3, Metroid Prime, and Vice City.

These are not casual gamers. I'm talking about people who have in some ways actually become the game they are playing. Their lifestyle is one of mortal combat, propelled by the adrenalin rush released in the virtual battles they fight online.

Some observers ask if we are losing our young men to video games. It's a serious question. The distinction between the game and real life has nearly disappeared for some. You've heard it said perception is reality. In a way, no matter what someone else determines to be real, the realm in which a person works out the meaning of their life is reality because what they wrestle with, what occupies their energy and attention, is what makes them who they are. Whether it's in the three-dimensional world of tangible objects, engaging the challenge of flesh and blood existence, or the virtual reality engineered by software designers and projected on a digital monitor, the contests of our lives capture our imaginations.

"Where your treasure is, there will your heart be also." (Matthew 6:21) What is anyone's treasure? A win? A score settled? A height surmounted? A challenger vanquished? A love won? The game is the sign of what's real, what's most important that consumes, what defines the meaning of the life of the gamer.

Tattoos are like the military emblems worn by warriors that tell of their service, rank, number of kills, and how the owner of the tattoo sees himself. This huge gaming phenomenon, with its concentration on fighting and triumphing over the enemy, is one more way that the archetypal themes and dramas of life are being lived out every day. Whether in online games, underneath tattoos, international negotiations, or daily life, I think everyone is engaged in distilling the meaning and purpose of his or her life.

Psychologists tell us that at various stages of life—and sometimes throughout our entire life—either we are trying to defend against a devouring mother, a tyrannical father, or a threatening monster. Or we are searching for the good mother, the good father, or the God who triumphs over the worst monster of all—death without end. These contests and quests fill our dreams, our careers, our family relationships, and everything we do. But we need weapons to fight the good, noble, and essential fights of our lives.

Even the New Testament says that weaponization is part of the character of human experience. Not as a way to participate in evil or vengeance, but to identify and conquer them. Look at this selection from the Apostle Paul's letter to the early church in Ephesus, just a short distance from the modern-day cruise port of Kusadasi, Turkey:

Put on the full armor of God, so that you can take your stand against the devil's schemes. For our struggle is not against flesh and blood, but against the rulers, against the authorities, against the powers of this dark world and against the spiritual forces of evil in the heavenly realms.

—Ephesians 6:11–12

Is the God of the Bible promoting a form of spiritual tattooing using the image of body armor? Perhaps this is the more important question: Is the darkness that many people struggle with, and sometimes wear the signs of, a race to the bottom, to the abyss where they are sure to meet their destruction? Or is their struggle instead the most necessary Mortal (and *spiritual*) Kombat against what they fear is their greatest threat as a way to triumph over it in a race to the top?

Many people became weaponized because someone let them down, creating an indescribable wound that drives everything they do, consciously and unconsciously. They hide behind walls, masks, and tattoos that keep others away while they walk through what feels like the valley of the shadow of death. Others have weaponized themselves with a shroud of darkness to show they know the way to the place where they must do battle in order to really live. No evil can take them unaware because they are fighting the heroic fight that every threat to their existence demands. The tattoos that signify these realities aren't pretty. The fight never is.

Above: This bright faced woman asked the artist, a friend, to create something that reflected her personality. Notice the skull that lurks behind the gentle flower.

Above: Soft and beautiful, this young woman revealed that some of her "stick and poke" tattoos have a prison look, and that gives her "an edge."

Above: Internationally-known blues man, Nick Moss, wears a tattoo of his angelic dog, Muddy, where all can see it.

Chapter 5: She Walks in Beauty

She walks in beauty, like the night
Of cloudless climes and starry skies;
And all that's best of dark and bright
Meet in her aspect and her eyes;
Thus mellowed to that tender light
Which heaven to gaudy day denies.
—George Gordon, Lord Byron, 1813

A single mom, this woman's tattoos convey strength, power, and beauty to her young daughter.

An analogy

A cathedral is a place of worship that evokes in me the otherworldly realm of the spirit and dimensions of the divine. The cathedral beautifies what would otherwise be a sparse space with massive columns, voluminous heights that amplify the slightest sound, and sweeping arches that seem to hold up the sky. Regardless of your belief you simply can't be untouched by the striking grandeur and beauty that lifts the heart, mind, and spirit in an entirely different way than almost any other kind of building does.

A cathedral is a dressed-up church. Age only deepens her beauty. She houses whispered secrets and stands strong as protective mother to her children. Her gardens sprawl beyond her walls like the train of a bride's gown. Everyone sees her glory from far away and is reminded that beauty can last, hold an impressive history, and still take our breaths away, even after hundreds of years.

And then there are her windows. Oh my! As the sun arcs from dawn to dusk, her stained-glass panes illuminate the cathedral's many charms as shafts of color alight on the many facets of her interior. If you're lucky, you too may be washed by a sweeping beam of light.

A cathedral's beauty is much like a woman's—in her body, her soul, and her mission to give life. The way she is adorned can be breathtaking, and deeply appreciated.

Once women used clothes, accessories, makeup, hair, and shoes—always the shoes!—to draw attention to their charms. But something is different in our time. Women are scribing tattoos on their skin (often, I assume to their mothers' horror) to enhance their beauty. Some are delicate and subtle. Others are strikingly bold. Like the stained-glass windows of a cathedral, the tattoos that women wear stimulate the senses. They stir the spirit, and often leave observers stunned. A woman's tattoos seem to have an almost mystical power over both her and her admirers. As social archeologists dig into our era hundreds of years from now, what will they make of the profusion of tattoos and those that women wear?

A man's tattoo is often about virility, strength, recovery, brotherhood, humor, a warning to stay away, worldliness, adventures, sports, or the memory of a beloved person who died. But most of the time a woman's tattoo tends to be about beauty, art, flowers she sends to herself, unhealed wounds, relationships, poetry, or lost/unrequited love. Do you hear the difference in what the two sexes are emphasizing? I believe a woman's nature fundamentally includes the inexplicable ability to bring beauty into the world. Think of it: Only a woman is able to birth new life. Is there anyone who isn't filled with pure joy and warm love when they see a newborn baby? A woman needs to believe that she is beautiful, and to experience that she is seen by others that way, not only in her body, but in all she is.

Have you noticed how large—exponentially bigger—the women's clothing section is in department stores compared to the men's? The size of the cosmetic space in CVS compared with the cologne space for men? When she was four years old I asked my daughter to come to Home Depot with me. She looked up at me and said, "Daddy, is there anything pretty there?" Women desire to be beautiful.

My wife Deb is a high school art teacher and an astounding, gifted potter. She has a studio in our house. If she can throw some clay on her wheel, I've discovered that she will give up sleep, food, social time, and even wild dance parties just for the chance to create something beautiful and new. It's as though she becomes the piece as she creates it. And when I hold one of her creations in my hand, enjoying a cup of coffee, I am holding a piece of her.

Is there anyone more obsessed with beauty than a woman? Whether it's her own person, her home, or her family, no detail is too small. Where does this come from? I think it comes from her creator. God seems to have endowed women with His love of beauty. Women have been given the gift to inspire, create, nurture, and be beauty for the enjoyment of everyone. When deep-sea divers find neon-fluorescent, spiraling jellyfish in the inky darkness of the ocean, when scientists confirm the uniqueness of every snowflake, when the Hubble telescope captures heart-stopping displays of planets and galaxies, we catch glimpses of a God who is obsessed with beauty. Women have received the divine ability to bring beauty into the world, and they can't stop themselves.

I remember the last conversation I had with Mabel in the nursing home. I asked her poor little bent over body what she needed. She answered, "My fingernails painted." When she passed, her daughters gathered to choose her dress and do her hair and nails for the final viewing before she was buried.

In the middle of a research conversation I've often asked a woman, "Did your father tell you that you are pretty and beautiful?" Too many said "No." When a girl hears she is pretty, or a woman hears "You're beautiful," it's not a shallow compliment to the self-absorbed preoccupation of the so-called weaker sex. Men need to pay attention to this: Telling the woman in your life that you see her as the very essence of beauty speaks to the core of her being. Doing this transmits value and worth to her soul, which she has received from the heart of her creator. When her unique beauty is denied, ignored, marred, or disfigured, a woman suffers indescribable pain. It may not be immediately evident, but it can live longer than her lifetime in the generations that follow her.

In this season in history, many women in Western culture are adorning themselves with messages, designs, stories, love, and mysteries on the canvas of their living skin. For many it is a way to express their essential beauty. The previous generation exfoliated their skin. This generation is writing on it. Women are still getting perms, but on their skin instead of their hair.

It's as though the souls of women have been pent up, spring-loaded, waiting for airtime. Their need to be beautiful and to express this fundamental essence of who they are has exploded onto the surface of the skin—sometimes hidden, in a secret place, and sometimes displayed boldly for everyone to see, feel, and deal with its impact. Whether a small but elegant chapel or magnificently adorned cathedral, a woman is beauty. She longs to express and to have her essence be cherished and enjoyed. Beauty is not only in the eye of the beholder, it resides in her heart from which it springs.

Message in a bottle

I met Constance outside a steakhouse in Raleigh, North Carolina. She was in her late twenties, and appeared to be waiting for someone. I noticed her beautiful tattoos, colorful and unique. I walked up to her.

"I like your tattoos. May I ask you a question?" She nodded a yes. "What does that one mean?" I pointed to a tattoo draped over her shoulder that ran half-way up her neck. It was a vessel with a letter tucked inside. The message was small and hard to read, but a magnifying glass would have solved my problem.

"It's a message in a bottle," she said.

"Would you tell me more?"

She said it was a message to her soul mate, whoever he was, and wherever he might be. "It will be his way of finding me."

She said that her tattoo "would call him in" and would be the way for her to know his authenticity, since the man with the ability to read it would know that it was she he was looking for. I was reminded of the story of Cinderella. In this case Prince Charming would have to find the woman whose message he could read and know it had been written for him.

"So your tattoo is about finding love?" I asked.

"Maybe," she said. "More about love finding me, and I'll wait for as long as he takes. But it would be nice if he could come soon!"

"Thanks so much, Constance. I hope he will come and find you soon, too." Her ride pulled up and she disappeared.

I am beautiful

It seems that some tattoos come from deep within, while others come from outside. Tattoos that come from within seem to match the person and work with the topography of their body, like a well-planned landscape designed by a thoughtful architect. These tattoos have interwoven elements, complimenting hair and eye color, and the size and proportions of the person.

Of course a woman is more than the sum of her tattoos, but they are windows, delicate stained-glass panes, that allow an observer to see into her soul. Patient thinking goes into the development of her tattoos, because she knows her life is a quilted, many-layered story. It has not come into being all at once. Her tattoos are pleasing to look at. They often flow like a poem or singing stream. They speak of how she loves herself and others. And even when they sometimes speak of abuse and abandonment, women's tattoos seem to reveal their heart-wrenching truths in amazingly sensitive, thoughtful designs. Perhaps the tattoo expresses the painstaking work a woman has undertaken in piecing together the delicate elements of a story that must be handled with the utmost care.

While I was enjoying a meal at a Vietnamese restaurant in Richmond, Virginia, Tinsely walked past me. She was a creature of rare beauty. Now, I know that according to unspoken social norms men who are in any kind of couple relationship—dating or married—are supposed to deny that they notice the beauty of any other woman on the planet. But that's just plain foolishness. Appreciating beauty is not the same as lust. Ever hear a group of women when they see a beauty? They carry on as free as you please, but God help the man who says what he is thinking. So, let's stop the pretending, shall we?

Did I say beautiful? Tinsely was drop-dead gorgeous. I knew I would never see her again. So as I often do when the moment is ripe, I got up from my pho noodle bowl and hurried after her, even though it's never easy way for a middle-aged man to approach a beautiful young woman. I was seriously interested in her tattoos. Not just that, but the relationship between her tattoos and her obvious beauty.

Once I caught up, I awkwardly explained that I research tattoos and the people who wear them. Would she sit with me as I ate lunch? Even as I uttered those innocent words my head was saying, "That is the lamest come-on this girl has ever heard in her life. Do you think she's an idiot!?" To my shock and amazement, she agreed, so I ordered a new round of summer rolls, which she objected to at first, but then joined in.

Her tattoos were stunning. She had brilliant leopard spots on her chest, arms, and legs. I asked, "Your tattoos ... can you tell me about them?"

At this time I was still at the bottom of my interview learning curve. I didn't want to blow the opportunity to really connect with her by rushing into something that takes time. And I surely didn't want to be heard as subtly mocking her, and wind up scaring off this fragile moment. So, I told myself to be patient, to wait, to let the interview happen. I didn't want to lead the outcome. I simply wanted her to say anything, and without any direction from me. Her words started slowly and introspectively.

"Leopards are shy beauties, unless you threaten them. If you do ... they can easily kill you," she began.

I waited, still feeling awkward.

My mind flashed to a trip I'd taken to Kenya some years earlier. I was on a safari in the Rift Valley. For five days our guide tried to find a leopard. Though my daughter and I saw thousands of animals including wildebeests, zebras, elephants, buffalo, ostriches, crocodiles, hippos, and even a gazelle hanging high in a tree, we never saw a leopard. But right here, at the table in the Vietnamese restaurant in Richmond, it felt like I was experiencing that rare leopard sighting. I watched, listened, and waited, carefully attentive.

Tinsley spoke again, "When something gets stolen, you make sure it doesn't happen again. You can't be tricked." She told me the gruesome story of how she was trafficked for sex in Canada, and later rescued. The leopard's wisdom, cunning, and readiness became emblematic of Tinsely's new life now that she was free. And that freedom had to be guarded. I couldn't help hearing what she said as a sermon to herself, illustrated by her soul in the leopard tracks on her skin. They came from within her.

Her parting words were, "I am beautiful, and don't you forget it!"

I stood, bowed, and hugged her. We smiled, then she was off.

The unexplored frontier

Then there are tattoos that seem to arrive on the skin from outside of the person. When someone is sexually abused at a very young age, a large part of their childhood is stolen. In its place are planted the wild brambles of lifelong fears that constantly tear and wound the heart. The innocence of childhood spontaneity and curiosity is enveloped by a convulsively troubled heart. The soul that has been wrongly touched is robbed of its ability to explore or experience free, joyful play. It can no longer dance in the rain because it must be constantly vigilant to protect the heart from being at risk ever again.

To me, when a tattoo comes from outside a woman's being, it seems out of sync and awkwardly placed on the body. This kind of tattoo looks like an isolated message, floating in space, disconnected from the soul. She is saying something about what happened, but she has not integrated the experience—good or bad, and most often bad. Her tattoo seems to come from a place she has been but does not know how to embrace as part of her experience. And so the image sits there, detached, disconnected, like something that does not belong. Even so, it is a statement about how she thinks and feels about what happened. She is not fully free to raise her voice or to be heard. Something is amiss, but she does not know exactly what. She is afraid.

I spotted Lisa in the cigar shop where I was killing some time. She looked confused, as if she felt out of place. Overwhelmed, she just stood there staring, almost paralyzed—like I would be at a woman's shoe store. "Need help?" I asked. I bet she thought I worked there.

"Yes, I need a nice cigar for my Dad."

I didn't have the heart to tell her that cigars are bold, smooth, even egotistical, but not necessarily "nice." Just then, a genius thought struck me.

"I will take you to the best cigar here if you let me ask a few questions about your tattoos."

"Okay," she said, hopeful that she had been rescued from her dilemma.

I took her to my favorite cigar—a Nicaraguan core with a Connecticut wrapper. "Smooth baby," I thought to myself. She bought the cigar and a special torch lighter to match. This was sure to make the old man happy. Making good on her promise since I'd fulfilled mine, we sat down in the leather chairs to talk.

Lisa's tattoos were cryptic, very hard to read, and to my untrained eye, looked like a mismatch with the person wearing them. "What does that one mean?" I asked, pointing to her triceps.

"It's a scarecrow," she said. "As a little girl I was always scared that birds would come and poke my eyes out. It's what my older sister told me when we were growing up. As I got older the fear grew stronger, so I got a scarecrow tattoo. Sometimes it works, and the birds stay away … and sometimes it doesn't work."

I asked about the tattoo on the back of her calf.

"Oh, that's a sand lizard that lives in the Arizona desert. It's what I remembered from the time my parents got divorced when I was about 6 years old."

We talked about the birds and the divorce and tiptoed toward her fears. As comfortable as I am with most people, I know it can be jarring for them to hear their own words. Sometimes that's all they can say because the depth of emotion related to long-forgotten experiences is so great. I've learned to sense when it's okay to go further and when it's not. Lisa had arrived at the border of a wilderness she couldn't venture into. So, I eased her back away from the unexplored frontier by thanking her for helping me. She pleasantly thanked me for the same and quickly left the smoke shop. I went back to buy the same cigar I'd suggested to her.

Wall of separation

I met Charity in a parking lot outside of Lowes. As she walked toward me to enter the store I saw four little faces of children across the top of her chest. They were so evidently on display they would be impossible for anyone to miss. "Wow, I like your tattoos," I said.

She stopped for a second. "Thanks. They're my grandkids. I'm not allowed to see them, and it's been four years. So this is the closest I can get." With that, Charity turned and walked away.

The things people tell me! It wasn't hard to imagine a half-dozen scenarios that gave rise to her family's breakup. But the details don't really matter as much as the wall of separation erected between Charity and her grandchildren. Sounds like a place poisoned with pain. Think about that pain. She endured it after the separation; she endured it when she sat to be inked with their smiling young faces; and she endures it now! Charity wears her wounds.

"Love bears all things, believes all things, hopes all things."
(I Corinthians 13:7) God bless you Charity, and the people on the other side of that wall.

Complications and connections

A woman's skin is beautiful. It can also be complicated. Who owns it? I would certainly say she does, although if my daughter had gotten a tattoo at the age of 18 I wouldn't have been happy about it. Still, I think a young woman is old enough to make the decision to tattoo herself and has earned the right to live with buyer's remorse. I've run into many who said it seemed like a good idea at the time, but had outgrown it, and wished they hadn't inked. Different seasons of life bring new ideas, values and struggles. Wouldn't it be nice if we could just figure out one multidimensional all-purpose, all-season life tattoo suitable to be worn from cradle to grave! What would you choose?

Sitting in tattoo studios, I've seen young women come through the door together with a group of friends, swirling excitedly, nervous with questions before going under the needle. "Will you tell your mom?" "What will your dad say?"

When I interview dads and moms, and grandparents of young women who were tattooed, they have a reluctant, measured, and mostly unhappy response. After all, they felt it was their job to carefully steward that skin during their girls' formative years. Teens don't understand much about why their parents say and do the things they do. Why should the subject of whose skin it is be any different?

There were hardly any adults I talked to who believed they owned their children's skin. But what they were dead certain about was that their daughters and granddaughters couldn't begin to appreciate the long-term consequences of the decision to get a tattoo—just as boys who go out binge drinking when they turn the legal drinking age can wind up dead from alcohol poisoning. Parents know that their girls don't understand what they might have to deal with later on because of their tattoo. But that's the difference between adults and kids. Those of us old enough to be adults see it from both sides now.

A lot of parents wondered if they had done something wrong by not interfering when their daughters pressed them to get a tattoo. A few reacted as if it were their own skin that had been violated in some way. In most cases the adjustment to having a tattooed daughter was made. Not without some lingering regrets, but most parents got over it. "It's water over the dam. Can't do anything about it now."

Still, I heard a lot of questions from parents and grandparents who wonder whether their beautiful girls had unconsciously sabotaged their future by limiting the number and kind suitors they would get since some men wouldn't want to marry a girl with too many tattoos. This concern didn't seem to bother any of the girls, at least for the moment.

I was dumbfounded by how many women get a tattoo as a fashion statement. No matter how much I looked for a deeper meaning or story in their tattoo, there was none. I became convinced that for some getting a tattoo was simply a fashionable accessory and nothing else. Granted, I'm a man and I am probably missing something that makes sense to the women who wear tattoos as fashion. If they are removable, I get it. Fashion does come and go, but it's a lot harder to get take a tattoo off than to put one on. And if that's the case, why go to the trouble to ink yourself today when you'll be out of fashion tomorrow? Is this trend a window into the "here and now" focus that a lot of our society is expressing?

One wise soul said "Keep your friends close, but your enemies closer." For some women, tattoos speak of their shame. The body-shaming streak in our culture has gotten completely out of control. It is very damaging, not only to the people who are its obvious victims, but to those who do the shaming. Our daughters, wives, and women friends are fighting back... some by killing themselves to become the idealized image dictated by others, and others by repudiating the false ideal. Some do it with tattoos.

Notice that the tattoo phenomenon exploded onto the scene after the Barbie doll's unattainable body image was planted into the psyche of the girls who dressed, played school, and vicariously dated Ken with their Barbie. Women's desire to become Barbie and men's desire to have and use Barbie has metastasized into a porn-addicted culture. This is what our young boys and girls are growing up in. It takes an enormous toll on everyone, especially on the self-image which has been stained before it has hardly become self-aware.

If the idealized body that both women and men want is one extreme, the other is obesity. America is not only addicted to sex, but to food as well. At the same time that we are chasing the unattainable ideal body, we are drowning in an overindulgence of food. This seemingly inescapable dilemma has ensnared our girls from the youngest ages. Many women embrace the sexualized culture through erotic tattoos, sometimes responding in extreme ways with tattoos on their breasts, face, or genitalia.

Past, present, future

Janice was walking down the street in Silver Spring, Maryland, as I passed her in my car. You know what comes next. Exactly. "I need to talk with her," I thought. I found a place to park a block away and quickly walked back to the area where I'd seen her.

She was tattooed from head to toe, full of multicolored words and symbols. I found her at a Starbucks, sitting with a friend. Walking up to initiate what I hoped would be a great tattoo interview I said, "Excuse me. I'm doing research on tattoos and I was wondering if I could take a second and ask you a few questions."

"Sure. But I don't have much time," she replied.

I got right to it. "You have a lot of beautiful tattoos."

"Thanks. I'm an artist in grad school with an emphasis in mixed media at the Savannah School of Art in Georgia."

You know what comes next: my standard question. "Can you tell me what your tattoos mean?

"They mean a lot of things." She said enthusiastically, explaining image after image to me. "This is the date I was born and so the sunrise means my beginning. This tattoo is for my brother who is in the army and I want him to stay alive and come back home. It's a prayer for him. This is my dog who passed away and the bone that made him happy.

These are the stars and planets in the galaxy. I hope my father is in it, waiting for me when it's my turn to die one day. These are the faces of strong, independent women who think for themselves and can make their own decisions."

This was amazing, like being on a tour in an art museum with a personal guide.

"My whole sleeve on my left arm is picturing flowers that you find in Italy. I want these to be part of my wedding one day. My leg has messages to God. See the woman leaning in with her ear toward heaven? It's saying, 'If you can send me a message I will listen.' This little girl here is my daughter who I gave up at birth. I'm not sure where she is, but I think about her every day."

Then she paused, thoughtfully as if wondering if she should go on. "I guess I can show you."

"Show me," I said. She turned away and lifted her shirt to show me the angel wings stretched across her entire back.

After a moment she dropped her shirt and turned to face me again. "I'm hoping to be an angel one day and help people. Maybe then I can go and find my dad, too."

I was in awe. But it didn't stop. Like the layers of meaning that I almost always discover under a tattoo that speak of the layers of experience and logic that are baked together in a person's soul, Janice took me to a new one.

"You know, I also struggle with depression, so sometimes I get a tattoo to pull myself out of it. I get a high from the needle that lasts for weeks. Call me crazy, but it works for me."

And just like that, like a rabbit that stuck its head out of its hole for a brief moment then popped back inside, Janice jumped up and said. "Well, gotta go now." And she was gone. I hardly had time to say thanks.

"Wow, what just happened?" I thought.

This was an instance of almost too much information; not too much for me to hear, but too much to understand in the moment. There was a whole lot going on that could take someone with different initials after their name and a couch in their office months, maybe years, to begin to fathom. But my knowing her story isn't my preoccupation. I'm curious to know whether Janice knows herself.

There was such an honest freshness and energy about this girl, even now I ponder the may layers of her storied life. Most of us run into something that forces us to stop and think about what it means. But Janice seems to be tattooing every question, every aspiration, and her most vital concerns just as immediately and freely as the soul who keeps their treasured thoughts in their private diary. This one isn't under lock and key but proudly, unabashedly out there for anyone to read. But what is the story?

Primal questions

The many women who took time to tell me their tattoo stories were all so genuinely helpful in giving me insight into their lives. But they were also keenly aware of the potential for mocking and disrespect, even at subtle levels. Still, they wanted to tell their stories, they wanted me to know the meaning behind their tattoos. Whatever the circumstances of each precious life, the unique images with which they chose to be inked were directly tethered to these primal questions I heard in every story:

Am I loved?
Am I capable of love?
Will I find love?
Will love come back to me?

When they explain their tattoos, they are surprised to discover even more meaning. The tattoos seem to continuously give up more hidden information when their owners are acknowledged and engaged by someone who listens respectfully, with an open ear wired to an open heart. Isn't that what so many of us want, with or without a tattoo? And beneath all the tattoos of the women I've explored, I found the curator of her own cathedral who seeks to design pretty stained glass windows that tell of her beauty, and her tireless passion to create more and more of it for as long as her life allows.

By now it might have occurred to you to wonder if I am pro-tattoo. I honestly can't answer that question if the only options are yes or no. What I think, what I do know, is that I have acquired a genuine respect for each person's life and whatever it is that inspired, compelled, or forced them to express themselves using a tattoo.

I love their tattoos because their images have become a way that I've gotten to know and love them. Many have become my friends. I cherish the time they've given me to research who they are. Most of all I am humbled by the gift of themselves. It continues to be an amazing, life-changing experience for me. I've reconsidered a lot of what I thought I knew and understood about life because I've risked hearing what's on the inside, beyond the signs that attracted my attention on the outside.

You know, tattoos have given these women a tool that has allowed us to talk to one another, bypassing a lot of the social awkwardness that often holds strangers apart from one another. I'm glad for that.

Above: This drummer wears a tattoo that says: "A father's love is forever."
His daughter has the same tattoo on her arm.

Right: This man sports a tattoo of 1950's pinup model, Bettie Page. He says that he's always admired her because she led the way for women to pose.

Above: A picture of youthful innocence, this young woman had a flower tattooed on her back to show her love for her mother.

Chapter 6: Tattoos are totems

Now defined as art, the totem has lost cult, taboo, and custom. Totem poles and wooden masks no longer suggest tribal villages but fashionable drawing rooms in New York and Paris.
—Mason Cooley

Featured on 26 History Channel shows, the heroic and highly decorated 1st Sgt. William "Bo" Bodette served in the Marines for 23 years. Many of his tattoos reflect his service in the military. His wife, Shelly, has been getting tattoos for the last 29 years. She says they tell the story of her life.

Geronimo (1829–1909) is one of the best-known American Indians, a medicine man of the Bedonkohe band of the Chiricahua Apache. He symbolizes the strong pride and rich heritage of the first Americans. Leading small bands of warriors, Geronimo was legendary for his 36-year resistance to US and Mexican military campaigns. Generations of Apache began fighting for their survival in the 1500s when Mexican and Spanish settlements were established in the American Southwest. Geronimo was the last and most famous of the Apache leaders to defend his people and culture before surrendering to the United States.

Extending over many generations, the war fought by the Indians against Mexico and the United States became more and more brutal. Geronimo was one of the most feared Indian leaders not only for his extraordinary military strategy, but his ability to see into the future. Leading sometimes as few as 30 skilled, loyal warriors, he conducted some of the most gruesome raids in the centuries-old campaign.

Three times, Geronimo surrendered to US marshals, but escaped from captivity twice. At one point, a quarter of the army's forces were hunting for him. In 1886 he surrendered for the last time. Still, less than 10 years later, he was celebrated by many Americans as a folk hero. In 1905 he published his autobiography, which he dedicated to President Theodore Roosevelt. That same year, Roosevelt invited him to his second presidential inauguration, and during their private meeting Geronimo again pressed unsuccessfully for his people to be return to their native lands in Arizona. Four years later, Geronimo died, still a prisoner of war, regretting that he had not fought to the end.

Legend has it that early in his life Geronimo's tribe gave him a *totem*. Derived from the Ojibwe *odoodem*, which means "his kinship group" totems are objects or animals with spiritual significance that also serve as emblems. Geronimo's totem characterized him as an eagle, a fox, a grizzly bear, and the wind. These were apt representations of his personality, wisdom, cunning, bravery and skill. His totem was his identity.

The tribes of the Pacific Northwest were the creators of totem poles. These red cedar towers sometimes stretched as high as 45 feet tall. They were carved with images and symbols of animal totems, symbols of protection that served as reminders of tribal, clan, and personal identity. Every shape and color had meaning. Carvers would often hide delicate secrets in the wood for future generations to discover.

The first poles were used to support family homes. In time they were decorated to reflect family legends, animals, people, and historical events. The scholar Eddie Malin has proposed that totem poles developed from these house posts, becoming funerary containers, memorial markers, and eventually symbols of clan or family wealth and prestige.

The poles were not worshipped, but they inspired respect and spoke of meaning, order, origin, and destiny. A totem pole's carved symbols were often translated into images painted onto the skin, akin to a family crest, providing a constant message of identity, purpose, and belonging that could be seen by the entire village. A person's identity derived from his family's totem pole.

Personal identity was at the root of Indian culture. Elders sent their children into the forest to watch for the animal that would become their spirit guide. For the rest of their lives they would emulate the animal's character and instincts. Some tribes believed that animals lived within each person, physically and spiritually, to serve as teacher, guide, and companion throughout their journey on earth. Discerning one's spirit guide, as these animals were known, was not a matter selecting a favorite animal. Rather, it was becoming aware of the animal the person most often saw, encountered, or was drawn to, whose character traits the person most identified with.

In Geronimo's totem, his animals symbolized a connection to the creator, intelligence, and courage (the eagle); cunning, quick wit, and diplomacy (the fox); and instinctiveness, power, and sovereignty (the grizzly bear). His totem also included wind, a powerful protective symbol. The wind was considered a living force, capable of communicating with those who could hear it. From this unique blend of characteristics, Geronimo learned who he was.

Like totems in American Indian culture, I see tattoos that frequently serve the same purpose. People often borrow images from the natural world, to create artful, moving, mystical pictures that signify their own identity.

Who am I?

Every part of this glorious world seems interconnected by God's design. The clouds teach abstract painting and forecast the future, cats teach us to land on our feet when we fall, and ants demonstrate the effectiveness of teamwork. An owl's patient, poised perch symbolizes wisdom; a beaver's industrious work informs us about the importance of planning; a tree, the virtue of stability that comes from having deep roots; flowers impart beauty; aloe plants provide healing; and the otter reminds us of carefree playfulness.

God has endowed all creatures great and small with unique identities, characters, and attributes, and He has done the same for human beings. Each created soul is fearfully and wonderfully made, no two like any other. But while an ox will never wonder about its purpose and meaning, God has given people the ability to reason and discern who they are.

As I have traversed the country, interviewing thousands of people who wear tattoos, I've discovered that one reason they are writing on themselves is to answer this question of identity. Who am I? How am I unique? What is my purpose in life? More than has ever been seen before in mainstream culture, people are expressing that search by trying on the totems available to them in tattoos.

The funny guy

I was in Cambridge, Massachusetts, speaking at a conference for pastors. I stayed in a private home. One morning I walked out on the porch to discover a very tattooed postman delivering the mail. Both legs, both arms, and his neck were covered. "This is not your father's mailman, I thought."

It was summer and he wearing the US Postal Service–issued shorts. Slung over his shoulder was the regulation leather bag holding the mail. From my few seconds of observation, I could see that he was quick and methodical and quick at his work. I thought his totem must be the beaver.

As usual, to begin a conversation with someone I spot as a prospective research subject, I say something brilliant like "Hey! Nice tattoos!" (Full disclosure: Most people who hear that look at me and keep on moving. Stories like this one are only a small sampling of those who stopped and waited to see what would happen next.) To my surprise, when I commentated on his tattoos, busy as he was, the tattooed postman stopped.

I learned that instead of the industrious beaver, the theme of his tattoos was that of a court jester. You know, the guy a few centuries ago whose job it was to make the king laugh. A bad joke or one that hit the king sideways, could have deadly consequences. As we talked, the postman walked me through the his family tree of comics and court jesters. And he proudly told me that to his knowledge every one of them had lived to a ripe old age.

He had already stopped to talk with me for five minutes, which is a lot of time for a postman. But I had to ask, "Are you a jester?"

Without skipping a beat, he sprung into a silly pose on one leg and announced, "I have a secret sauce I use to keep my coworkers from going postal! My secret? Laughter."

And I laughed!

Though his job was delivering the mail, the postman's true identity is the funny man. I was struck by how clear he is about who he is. Secure in his identity, he lives his mission by bringing humor and joy to everyone in the court where he performs. He wears his totem well. It says exactly who he is. What a marvelous man.

The bad boy

Jimmy was in Starbucks. He was a muscled guy in a muscle shirt, sporting a gold chain around his thick neck. He looked like a cross between a Wall Street banker and a gym rat with tats.

"Hey, got a second?" I asked.

"Sure!"

"I'm researching tattoos. Can you tell me what you know?"

Jimmy was more than eager to fill me in. "Tattoos are chick magnets, man. I have babes all day walking up and asking me where I'm from. You know, chicks want a bad boy, whether they're 18 or 80!"

Then, slapping my arm, Jimmy said enthusiastically, "Hey, you should get some! Maybe it would help ya out!"

In hindsight, I think Jimmy misunderstood my question about tattoos. He was so confident in his status as a tattooed chick magnet that he thought I wanted to know how I could look like him, be like him, and reap the same rewards!

I was tickled by his unsolicited counsel, so I decided to see what else he might offer. "Do you really think it would help me?"

"You're probably a good guy, but you're also probably pretty lonely. Become a bad boy, man. See what happens!" And off he went.

For Jimmy there's a direct and unmistakable relationship between his tattoos and who he sees himself to be—the chick magnet. Whether he really is, or just imagines himself to be, I don't know. But the confident energy he expressed told me that Jimmy wants everyone, not just women, to see and experience him as the guy who scores all day, every day. Why? He wants everyone to know that being a bad boy means you're not lonely. And even if it only comes from people asking about his tats, he's right.

Search for identity

A lot of English surnames originally identified a person's occupation. Smith meant you were a metalworker or blacksmith. Miller was someone who worked in a grain mill. Taylor was a gentlemen's clothier. The name Clark derives from "cleric," or scribe. You can easily imagine the origins of Baker, Turner, Cook, Wood, Butler, Fisher, Mason, and Knight. My own last name is Dayhoff. I wonder if my character trait is taking days off?

It used to be that family, and the larger community of families, helped young souls find their identities. One purpose of the nuclear family is to provide a nurturing and supportive environment, so the growing child can experiment, try things out, and discover their own totem. God has created each of us to be wonderfully complex persons with particular attributes, genius, and skills. Every healer, wise man, artist, speaker, prayer warrior, businesswoman, builder, inventor, and astronaut is unique, and created with purpose. The trick of course for each of us is to find out who we are.

In our time, many people wonder if the once-reliable structures of society are broken beyond repair. These include marriage, the family, communities, government, and the church. As a result, many people search for their "totems" in other groups and experiences.

Despite the dramatic changes in the order of modern society people still long to experience themselves as having intrinsic value and worth. They still need to be a vital part of a group. The search for identity and meaning is as old as humanity. Today tattoos are a tool that more and more people are using to express their search for and announce their identity.

Within the tattoo community—those who create, get, and wear them—I have discovered this pattern: People try on different, but not necessarily dissimilar identities, to see if they fit. One way this is expressed is when a person acquires a variety of tattoos over time. It's like the painter who has an internal vision of what she wants to illustrate on the canvas in front of her. As each layer of paint, each shape materializes, she stops to ponder what she sees. She waits as inspiration and additional insight bubble up in her consciousness, then more color, density, shape, and size is added to the work.

There are few striking works of art I know of, be it a painting, sculpture, poem, or symphony, where the finished work was created in one sitting. While there are some notable exceptions, most breathtaking works of art are the result of repeated interior reflection and external action that adds, layer upon layer, to the story the artist is attempting to tell. Like all good and true stories, it is not one-dimensional, but varied and moving and alive.

What does that look like in a tattoo? The ones I've seen demonstrating this search for an identity that fits are cryptic collages, with many elements that are like points on a treasure map. Stopping at any one point lets you see what the tattoo wearer was experiencing and thinking at that time. But to stay there would be to miss the journey that the person who owns the tattoo is still on. Like life itself, these works of art mature, filling out the discovery of who we are. And if the amazing illustrations I see on people's skins are any example of the truth of their interior lives, then I can only conclude that we—all of us—with or without tattoos, are deeply complex, multidimensional souls whose very essences are themselves, reflections of the vast wonder of the God who gave us life, and breath, and skin, and imagination to exercise the grand privilege of plumbing the depths of our own existence.

Choosing an identity

I was hungry, so I went to a late-night pizza parlor in Cocoa Beach, Florida. A pretty, glowing, young woman, maybe 18 years old, took my order. She seemed to move at the speed of light, attending to multiple orders and paying customers, all with a smile. Her energy and movement were dizzying, making it hard to keep up with her, even though I was simply standing, waiting for my order.

She had loud tattoos that could not be missed. Her head was half-shaved and also tattooed. Both arms had sleeves and her calves had big tattoos of rabbits. In fact, her whole body theme was rabbits: rabbit tracks, rabbit ears, lucky rabbit's feet, and rabbits with many different expressions. She even had the silly rabbit from the Trix cereal box! I decided to chat her up while I waited at the counter.

"Are you a rabbit, hon?"

"Of course I am," she said, moving back and forth as she did her work with rabbit-like quickness. "Rabbits are fun, silly, and fast. People love rabbits," she said with certainty. "You did know they are fast, right?"

"I do now! I think you're the first human rabbit I've ever met."

"Yep. Pretty special, huh?"

"Very special!" I said.

She spoke without stopping, doing several different tasks at once.

Before I knew it my slice of pizza had been served up. As I paid I caught her attention once more, "It was a joy to meet you, Rabbit."

She didn't correct me, just smiled and said, "Somebody tried to label me autistic. I chose rabbit instead, and I love it!"

Sometimes, maybe even a lot of times, other people try to tell us who we are. I suppose that's all well and good—for the person doing the labeling. But what about the person being labeled? It has to fit. Rabbit heard the word "autistic" and knew it didn't fit. It wasn't her as she knows herself on the inside. She took on the task of figuring that out, and landed on something that does fit. How do I know? She had a sense of delightful, radiant contentment. Her tattoos help her understand and communicate who she is.

Known by their seal

Tasting a glass of wine is a pleasure, especially if the wine has been perfected with the proper care and storage. Each bottle of wine has a seal at the top. An intact seal is proof that the integrity of the wine inside has remained intact too. Large chemical trucks have a seal to indicate that what's on the inside lives up to what is written about it on the outside.

The New Testament says that God's Holy Spirit is a seal on our hearts. The presence of that seal assures us that the treasured contents of His very presence remains within us, pure and undefiled. This seal is the evidence that we have a secure inheritance that we will eventually enjoy fully, even though in the physical realm we are threatened by death.

No matter what they are on, seals certify the quality of what they are protecting. There's a correlation between what is signified on the outside and what's on the inside.

John was about 87 years old. He shuffled past me as I opened the door to a diner. You could tell he was a regular when the waitresses shouted his name as he entered. His neck was bent down, and he couldn't look up. I followed behind him and started looking for a booth. As we rounded the corner we came upon a group of men, all sitting in good order. There were about 18 more 87-year-old Johns!

I was going to tell you that despite their age there was a natural and relaxed good humor. But I think it's actually because of their age—and experience—that anyone walking by would have been welcomed. I easily found myself talking with them. When I mentioned that I noticed two of the seats at their table were empty, they explained that these friends had just died in the past month. I was about to make a joke about escaping from their wives or the nursing home, but I was saved from my own stupidity. Instead, the old codgers hurled their own old man jokes, and they were far better than mine.

When the waitress came over one guy looked at her and said, "Jenny, I'd like to order a red-headed nurse with long legs." All the guys laughed.

John looked over at me and said, "Charlie puts the same order in every week, but we like to hear him say it."

Most of them had tattoos, blurry from many decades of life. I could see anchors, ships, airplanes, names of men, dressed women, flags, unit and company names from their fighting days. I felt like I'd stumbled into a rare find, a living WWII museum. Like some of the volunteer curators I've seen at actual museums, it looked to me that a lot of these guys were, without doubt, months away from dying, and they all knew it.

"Could you tell me about your tattoos?" I asked.

"Will you buy us lunch?" one guy quipped. They all laughed loudly, then it was quiet for a minute. "Why do you want to know?" the man in the wheelchair asked. I think he was scouting to see if I was there to secretly mock them.

"My dad served on the USS *Prairie* in the South Pacific. He never got a tattoo, and I always wondered why." Maybe being a navy brat would buy me something.

The guy who still had most of his hair piped up, "That's cuz he was never drunk like we were!" They all guffawed again. Humor opens up a lot of carefully guarded valuables.

Then came each man's story. "Here's my unit. Most of them died in the war. Now, I'm the only one left." The group got quiet, reverent, respectful.

Another man pointed to his shoulder, "This is my girlfriend. When I came home, she had already married another guy. She got tired of waiting."

"Hey! I get tired of waiting for you too, Jimmy," someone teased. More chuckling.

A few of the men were silent, staring off to another time or another dimension not easily spoken of. I suddenly felt like an killjoy, stealing their outing. Several more precious stories were told while I stood among them.

With sincere respect for what they'd given me, I looked at the group of wrinkled warriors. "God bless you men. My father would have loved to know you." I stood at attention and saluted, honored by their stories … and their lives. Some saluted back.

I made my way to a booth on the other side of the diner to savor the experience over lunch. Somehow, from fathers, grandfathers, uncles, and brothers, or from the accidents and incidents of life that propel us in directions we never thought possible, including becoming a warrior, each of these men had acquired their unique totem identity. The emblems they once wore on their uniforms, their seals as soldiers, and the scars from life's inevitable battles, were eventually etched as tattoos, telling the secrets of their souls. Underneath each seal the content of their character has aged to perfection. And it's proven, safe, and intact.

This is who I am

Slavery is one of the most diabolical devices ever devised to deny, steal, and control personal identity. From the second century BC to the present day, slaves have been branded and marked as property. To be a slave is to be whatever someone else—not you—decides you are. All slavery is the blasphemous theft of a person's freedom.

And yet, no matter what humiliation and depravity might be heaped upon some people, their bodies and minds tormented into apparent submission, their spirits valiantly fight for life. To the world they have are nothing. But an invisible identity in the deepest recesses of the heart inspires them to live on.

When human brutality becomes most perverse it does more than murder people. During the Holocaust that lasted from 1933 to 1945, millions of people were marked by the Nazis. Ripped out of society, they were systematically stripped of all value as people, culled out of society as if they were rodents and vermin. They were forced to experience the lowest form of human existence, first as a people marked by the yellow star of David, later as tattooed prisoners in concentration camps, and eventually as naked corpses dumped into mass graves.

Sign of ownership

I was in Charlotte, North Carolina, for a long day of meetings with other pastors, listening to their stories. I'm always stimulated by people's stories, but listening takes a lot of unseen energy. I was tired. When the day was over I thought, "Why not end the evening with a nice blues bar?" Notice I said not "at," but "with." A blues bar is not a place. It's an experience. I wanted a blues bar evening.

I looked up the Charlotte Blues Society and wasn't disappointed with the large selection. The bar I went to turned out to be in a falling down house! "Aha!" I thought. "Great blues music straight ahead." There could be no other reason people would come here.

The floors were uneven, which makes for good blues dancing. You move all over the place. The ceilings had glitter in the drywall mud. The last time this place saw a fresh coat of paint was in the 1970s. And the bathrooms were … well, they were tattooed!

I think this is more of a male thing, but I haven't checked with women to know for certain. It seemed like everyone who'd made a trip to the head in the last 10 years had drawn pictures and messages all over the walls, the ceiling, and even the toilet bowl itself. Such creativity! I could have spent some good research time exploring the hieroglyphics but decided to enjoy the music and the patrons instead.

The band was a group of men, sixty-somethings. The bass player was the only one standing, and he was grooving. The singer was a black woman, I'd guess about 40. She knew her stuff. Her voice and sway could take it to the river, let me tell you. The crowd could see her sweat as she sang, and we all liked it that way. She sang "Too Many Dirty Dishes in the Sink for Just Us Two." This was what I needed after an intense day of listening. It was time for my soul to speak, to sing, and dance. The music helps me do that.

When the band broke between sets I walked outside for some air. I saw a young woman dressed for sale. To be honest, I was afraid to speak to her. What if the police came? Would it look like a drug deal— or some other kind of deal—was about to happen? Was I walking into a trap?

Then I heard her, a voice that sounded like it could have been my daughter's.

"Where are you staying? Want some company?"

"Hon, I don't want company. But God bless you, child."

She was still for a moment, quiet. I stood there looking up into the night sky.

"My name's Tanya." She had stopped trying to sell me.

I noticed she had a tattoo. I asked, "What's that mean?" pointing to the image on her shoulder. It was a crown, like a king would wear.

"It's from my man."

"Your man's a king?"

"Yeah." Another moment of silence and then, "Are you really stupid, or are you just playing with me?" She didn't wait for an answer. "That's my man! He lets me work for him and we make money together. We all gotta do what we all gotta do, right?"

Now she was inviting me into her realm. I waited … seemed like there was more to come. And it did.

"We're gonna get married one day," she said, almost knowing the claim sounded as shallow as her offer to make me comfortable a few minutes earlier.

"Wow," I thought, "How'd you like to wear THAT for an engagement ring?"

She's sealed with the sign of her man, the one who's gonna make all her dreams come true. Only trouble with that is she has to live the nightmare first, maybe forever.

And what does that symbol of her man the king mean? "I'm his slave."

I gave her five dollars. I'm not sure why. It just felt right to tell her, in an admittedly coarse way, "You're worth something child, just because you are." I walked back inside.

Right: This bass player celebrates great blues men on his arm. B.B. King will be the next addition.

Left: This young man's tattoos reflect his connection with natural world.

Right: It took four years for this man to get the design his of tattoo "just right." The image commemorates his military service during Desert Storm and honors those with whom he served.

Lower left: Manny Yanes, bass player for Patti LaBelle for 15 years, wears religious and mystical tattoos on his arm.

Chapter 7: The Soul Needs Its Shaman

Shamanism is being reinvented in the West precisely because it is needed. —Michael Harner

A former painter and special education teacher, this extraordinary tattoo artist applies her aesthetic abilities to every piece she creates.

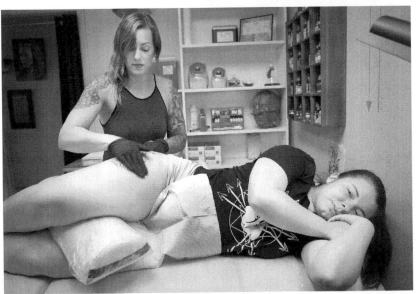

Tattoo artist, Pepper Raefin, says she spends at least an hour with every client to help them choose just the right image and steer away from those they may regret. This is a photo of Pepper working on a first-time tattoo for he 18-year-old niece, who chose a bouquet of flowers.

Sylvester Stallone's iconic screen character Rocky Balboa lives a classic American story that I love. He was an uneducated, working-class Italian-American boxer with a side-hustle as a debt collector for a seedy loan shark in the slums of Philadelphia. Rocky's luck changes when he gets a once-in-a-lifetime chance to go from a small-time back-alley fight club to a match with the champion, Apollo Creed. I love Rocky's girlfriend, Adrian, who couldn't bear to watch him fight. She was afraid for him. But most of all, I love Mickey Goldmill, Rocky's trainer.

Mickey had his demons, but he'd lived with them long enough to acquire some unexpected wisdom along the way. In one fight scene Balboa is bloodied and nearly blind from the unrelenting, pounding punishment. The bell brings the beating to a momentary halt. Rocky falls on the corner stool, barely conscious. He spits gunk, including a tooth, into a bucket. In that ugly moment, reduced to survival instincts, Mickey leans in and speaks mysterious words that ease Rocky's pain and give him the strength to stand and fight another round. It makes me wonder what life would be like if we all had someone like Mickey in our corner, guiding us in our most difficult hours. Mickey was Rocky's shaman.

Broadly speaking, a shaman is a wise man or woman with knowledge and insight derived from nature and the spirit world. Every indigenous culture has had shamans, most connected with nature, who channeled transcendent energies to impart wisdom, knowledge, and healing. Each culture and every religious tradition has its version of the shaman—the prophet, medicine man, witch doctor, priest, Christian mystic, and Russian *staretz*—have all mediated between the natural world and the world of the spirit to help others face life's most threatening challenges.

The new shaman

Ancient or modern, I am convinced that every soul wants to know the meaning of their existence. Some respond to this compelling desire by letting their soul write its stories on the skin. Most don't do that alone. For many people, the tattoo artist has become the new shaman.

Like a psychotherapist hearing a client wrestling with a problem, or a priest listening to a penitent heart, tattoo artists enter into a remarkable communion with their clients. In this exchange, experience and its meaning are chronicled in the images and words that appear on the skin. Often it takes over multiple sittings and extended periods of time, sometimes even years. It's a remarkable, intimate encounter that isn't repeated in any other experience I know of.

Popular culture has captured the archetypal search for spiritual insight to face the most difficult and consequential challenges in life. In the *Star Wars* series, the order of the Jedi knights includes polymaths, philosophers, and warriors who study, share, and become wisdom. Obi-Wan Kenobi and Qui Gon Jinn were two early masters of the living Force. Though they wished only to be ordinary, anonymous men, they confronted darkness by becoming Jedi knights. But even Jedi need a spiritual guide. Theirs was Yoda, who had been a Grand Master Jedi for 800 years. He trained almost every Jedi that came after him. The *Star Wars* universe speaks to us because it acknowledges what we sense—that there are layers of wisdom, and we need a shaman, a mediator who knows and can guide us in the way.

Gandalf the Grey is a wizard in *Lord of the Rings: Fellowship of the Ring,* one of J.R.R. Tolkien's tales about a fantasy world called Arda and Middle-Earth. Gandalf guides a small group of intrepid travelers through countless harrowing adventures. No matter the challenge, they were resolute in their commitment to see the struggle through to the end—the destruction of an evil, cursed ring. In one scene, after battling orcs and trolls, the group came upon a balrog, an ancient, giant fire monster standing more than a hundred feet tall. At the Bridge of Khazad-dûm, Gandalf entered the battle against the balrog to allow the others to escape. Gandalf refused the balrog passage by breaking down the bridge with his staff, only to be caught by the demon's whip and dragged to his death. Much later, the grieving team meets a glowing image that frightens them. The image turns out to be the reincarnated Gandalf the White. He earned his return passage to life over and over again as he faced death and indescribable evil to continue his service as the group's spiritual father. Tolkien's famed trilogy, written in the 1950s, has become wildly popular in our time in the movie adaptations because of the eternal truths the stories contain. One of them is that we need a spiritual father to help us navigate the most difficult parts of life.

From the interviews I've conducted with artists and those they ink, it's not an exaggeration to say that the tattoo artist has guided many travelers by building bridges that allow their clients to cross over into the pain of receiving the tattoo, and in so doing, into a greater knowledge of themselves.

I've sat in tattoo parlors for hours at a time—I think I've logged 20 full days by now—usually with people while they were getting their tattoos. I've noticed that the character and depth of the inevitable wincing from the pain of the imbedded tattoo needle was directly connected to the kind of conversation taking place. Darkness, pain, and tears often came when the person talked about the deep meaning of the images being drawn on their skin.

The tattoo shaman is comfortable in this space, drawing images on the skin while the client responds. There's something unique to this recipe. It's part emergency room doctor trying to control the pain, part therapist finding the core wound, part priest mediating spiritual solace, and part artist trying to find the image inside the soul that wants to be released onto the skin. What's the goal to all of this? It varies with everyone. But what I consistently witness is what looks like a search for understanding, meaning, integration—and most of all, for freedom.

Search for a missing childhood

Terry was getting a swarm of butterflies inked behind her right shoulder. There must have been more than 30 of them in various sizes and colors. I sat in front of her as the artist worked, her face screwed up in pain. At times she would tear up. A couple of times she said she was going to pass out.

Both Terry and her artist knew I was doing research. He was honored to have me witness this sacred exchange, between himself and Terry, his living canvas that they were illustrating together.

I asked about the butterflies. She said, "I think they're pretty, whimsical. and like flying flowers." When I asked if that was all they meant she began to cry. At first, I assumed her tears were from the pain of the needle. But I found out her tears were not coincident with the needle, but my question. The butterflies told Terry's life story.

She told me that her family was crazy … there were frequent police visits, drug busts, and her dad in handcuffs too many times to count. When she lived at home, she was suspended from school when her clothes smelled like marijuana, because her mom and dad were constantly high. All she wanted to do was escape, to fly away.

"Sometimes I had to sleep over at other people's houses because my parents were fighting. Other times there was no food in the kitchen … Owwwww!" This time it was definitely a response to the needle.

"My brother left, and I haven't seen him for five years. Nobody knows where he is."

The only thing to say when somebody's pouring their heart out is to acknowledge what you heard, that it registered with you.

I took a deep breath and let it out. "Whew, that's a lot, Terry. I get it. Thanks for telling me."

"I don't know why I told you all that crap," she said.

The pain, the skin, the tattoo artist, and the story were a sacred space where healing and hope were painted on her skin by someone she trusted to do it right. And I was privileged to hear the hurt in Terry's heart. Sometimes just knowing we're heard goes a long way toward helping us live with pain so that it isn't the focus of our living anymore. "Love covers the multitude of sins" that have wounded us.

Artist wisdom

One young man wanted to get tattoos on his face, but his new shaman resisted. He asked to see the young man's identification to verify he was of legal age. His advice to was to go home and really think about it. The young man snapped his ID back and said, "Never mind. I'll just go down the street and get it done somewhere else." And he did.

Another artist, Bob, told me, "Tattoos are one of the few rites of passage left, along with signing up for the military, drinking, and voting."

Confessional healing

One time, while I was observing a tattoo artist at work, I heard voices off to my right. A new client, Mary, sat with her artist. I kept my distance but could still hear her talking. It was like I was sitting outside a confessional but hearing every word the penitent and her priest were saying to each other.

She wanted to know if he could draw her childhood. The artist asked "What do you remember? What makes you smile? What was the most fun?" Mary took a moment, looking off in the distance as if she could see her past. After listening briefly I was surprised that the artist came up with a proposal so quickly. Maybe he was especially good at it, or maybe running the clock costs money … maybe both!

The artist worked his magic, creating a tattoo of children holding hands in a circle with colorful toys and dolls at their feet. I stayed for the two hours it took for this to happen. Mary was in obvious pain during the whole procedure, but through it her childhood returned and was alive on her skin.

When she got up to leave, I carefully stepped in her path. "Excuse me. I'm researching tattoos. I was wondering if I could ask a few questions?"

"OK, I guess. What do you want to know?"

"Your tattoo, it's beautiful. You must be a very proud owner."

I expected Mary would have echoed that sentiment after having just gotten such a beautiful image on her skin. But the moment suddenly turned solemn.

"I've thought about it for a long time," she said.

"What do you mean?"

"I spent most of my childhood sick and in the hospital. I had an immune system disorder thing going on. I couldn't play with toys or other children because of germs and other stuff."

"I'm so sorry, Mary,"

"No, it's okay." Glancing back at the artist who inked her, her mood brightened. "My artist brought me toys and children to play with today. So I'm good."

Her heart longed for lost joy. Mary and her shaman delved into the pain of her childhood and surfaced with an image that I suspect is restoring her soul.

Blind guidance

After spending so much time in tattoo studios, I was struck by the number of people who would just come in for a consultation before going all the way. Their inquiries weren't all that different from the initial meeting to ask a dentist about a tooth implant, a lawyer about a complex legal issue, or a counselor about getting into an awkward personal matter. I suspect the advice-seekers needed to establish a feeling of comfort about what they were about to do, and they were looking for a connection to the tattoo artist before they decided to place their life—and their skin—in his hands.

What really took me by surprise though were the people—usually young—who would just say to the artist, "Do my arm … whatever you think." Yes, that's right! They would allow the artist full license to permanently etch whatever she chose onto their skin, asking her, in effect, to impart a permanent influence over the rest of their lives.

Here's where the gift of the mediator really shines. The artists I saw were wise. They were able to intuit what the image ought to be. I watched them create a tattoo without seeking any further information from the customer. From my conversations with artists this is not an unusual request. Based on what I've witnessed there's a kind of sixth sense that gives them the ability to discern things about the people they ink that are right on the money, even though this information was not provided to them by their clients.

Were these seemingly chance encounters really random, or were they intended by a higher wisdom than we know? There are no satisfying answers within the three dimensions of this life. But clearly, there is another, fourth dimension, a spiritual realm that confers a host of abilities that enable people to do things they ought not be able to do.

Guidance through remembrance

As you might guess from the chapter about tombstones, the tattoo conversation between the client and artist often centers on a deceased person. The client doesn't want a face, or date, or cross, but something else that will memorialize their dearly departed. This is when the tattoo artist earns the shaman title. Think about it. A living person is calling on the memory of a once-living person, now dead, to be recreated and carried on their skin until their death!

I've heard artists ask questions like, "What did your dad love?" One time, a young man, Jimmy, had a really hard time putting his wishes into words. So, the artist asked, "What is your favorite memory of your dad?" Jimmy lit up talking about his dad's cherished 1954 Chevy, and how they worked on it together during his teens. Then, I watched as he got that car tattooed over his heart. That experience was a fond, fun, and precious memory that lived in his heart, but now also on his skin.

One day I decided to stop by a headstones and memorials business in Great Neck, New York. I sat in the parking lot waiting for several customers to go in, so I could overhear what the conversations sounded like. When I finally stepped inside, a 60-year-old man greeted me, saying he'd be with me in a few minutes. He was with somebody just then. Of course, I knew that. "Perfect," I thought.

He rejoined a lady in her eighties, I'd guess. She thumbed through a binder of tombstones and pointed to the one she wanted. The salesman asked for the dates of her husband's birth and death and how she wanted to pay. The whole transaction only took about 10 minutes and 35 words. This has long been a traditional way to bury and remember the dead. But I wondered, "Would anyone visit this tombstone? Would anyone ever see it?" I found myself hoping that when I graduate from this world that my children would consider picking a tattoo for themselves, and not a tombstone. I would be forever on their skin, and the right artist would guide them to the right tattoo.

The difference between the conversations the headstone salesman and the tattoo artist have with their clients is striking. Both involve a business transaction, but with the shaman/artist the conversations are careful, seeking inner thoughts, that often included an hour or more of just talking before taking any action. Unlike the headstone salesman, who I suppose would have been open to suggestions about a custom design—with a pricey upcharge, of course—the tattoo artist wants to know much more than dates and names. She listens to hear the person's soul.

A headstone marks the physical resting place of the deceased and will only be seen a very few times in the course of its duty as a silent sentinel to the dead. But a tattoo becomes part of you, is part of you. Yes, payment is made for the service rendered. But when you get out of the chair in the tattoo parlor you walk away with another part of yourself disclosed—to yourself, and to everyone else who sees you—whether they know what it is they are seeing or not.

When people cross the threshold of the tattoo parlor, leaving behind what some might call a life of undefiled skin, and sit to get inked, they often start the conversation with the artist by asking what his tattoos mean. A lot of artists have a lot of tattoos, so there's a lot to talk about. That conversation exposes the realm of the soul in both people that goes much deeper than what anyone will ever see on the outside. As I've listened to the back and forth between an artist and client, I've found myself thinking, "By the time a person gets their tattoo and begins to talk about it, maybe it's true that you can judge a book by its cover." Then again, I heard some older artists just make something up, because they decided that an 18-year-old kid who was a third their age couldn't possibly grasp what he would say if he told the truth.

Are there limits?

Freaks. That's the artist's word to describe a certain, let us say, genre of people who wear tattoos. Since they've gone mainstream, the shock value of your garden variety tattoo has evaporated. So those who want to be shocking go for extremes. Some tattoo their face, get horn implants like a devil, change their face to look like a cat, or in once case I've seen, a parrot. I found these so-called freaks in Tampa, Virginia Beach, and Seattle.

This is a group of extreme tattooed people who often come out at night and stay indoors during the daytime. Did they discover they couldn't bear the stares and fear they saw in people's faces? One guy didn't realize that the way he'd transformed himself scared the hell out of people until he saw a mother grab her frightened child and run away. Did they come to believe they didn't fit with the people of the day? Did they become even more self-conscious of their freakishness when faced with ridicule and isolation?

Most of the artists I talked to say that freaks are becoming a larger segment of the tattoo community. I've listened to a lot of them struggle with whether or not they want their art displayed on these people. So here's a clue to more about the nature and character of our tattoo artists: They care about how their work represents them, and they care about what is going in inside the people they ink. More than one said to me, "Freaks need a shrink and it's not me!"

The tattoo shaman seems to be able to discern people who may be experiencing a mental health crisis when things are so far outside the norm that they sense something is wrong. They aren't willing to participate in someone further marking themselves with dark or confusing messages that might only compound the person's drama, rather than relieve it.

There's another limitation I've been told most artists put on themselves—no hate tattoos. They won't ink profanity, the swastika, hate symbols, the middle finger, or phrases like "I hate_____." The artists get weary of hate messages. Most will gently ask the paying customer, "Do you really want to live with a hate tattoo for the next 50 years?" That doesn't mean they won't design flaming skulls and bleeding wounds. But artists understand those images to be an expression of emotion and color, not symbols of hate.

Despite my observation that most artists won't "go there" when it comes to hate and profanity, that doesn't go for all of them. I met a guy at a tattoo convention that had F**K YOU scrawled across his chest. He was mean. He told me how his anger was so deep that instead of flipping the finger at everyone, he just decided to say it all day, every day, to everyone. Eventually though, the satisfaction of telling off the rest of the world faded. As more and more people were pushed away by his message, he was left alone with himself and his message. In time his tattoo began to boomerang. It was as if he heard it saying F**K YOU to himself. And that nearly broke him. He had to come to terms with what was eating his soul that had floated up onto his skin.

Like all creatives, tattoo artists want and expect to get recognition. And I agree. The tattoo art medium has many famous practitioners who can charge upwards of $500 an hour for their unique branding. Some clients feel empowered and privileged to be inked by such people. They're proud to own and be part of a precious collection of art—on their skin. They value it as a priceless expression of self-awareness created by a unique collaboration. Just as the client's story lives on their inked skin, so the stories of both artist and client live in each other. Sometimes people believe their own intrinsic value increases as a result. I am told that some people leave permission, through their last will and testament, to have their tattoo cut off after death and framed for remembrance. I've checked online. There are businesses that specialize in this.

And just as works by famous artists work become much more valuable after their death, the work of tattoo artists is beginning to be treated the same way. They have talent, inimitable style, and unspeakable power.

We live in a time when the role of the traditional shaman—the priest, the holy man, the prophet, the wise one—has faded. We may need them now perhaps more than ever, but our culture has dismissed the significance of the unseen, intangible world, believing the answers to our most perplexing questions can be found through the independent exercise of our primary human endowment—the intellect. We don't want to depend on anyone else, and we have no idea what to do with the spirit realm.

The grandmother or village elder of times past was present during the precious moments when a child or young adult would ask questions about life, death, marriage, sex or how a broken spirit heals. Priests, rabbis, and pastors are harder to find today, and it's even harder to believe that they understand much about the world of ordinary people. They have either fled the scene or been forced out by a culture looking for something more than a philosophical discussion. People want to touch God directly. Do the traditional shamans criticize with their stern eyes? Are they viewed as being "out of it," detached from real life? Or have their gifts of discernment, wisdom, insight and guidance been summarily dismissed by a culture that takes pride in deciding what's right on its own?

Whatever the reason for shutting out the shaman, this doesn't satisfy our abiding need for the mystical wisdom that an extraordinary Mickey Goldmill, Master Jedi, or Gandalf the White can provide to guide us on our journey in life. For some who are still awake to their soul's desire for deeper meaning, they have found the tattoo shaman who is listening. Somehow, they mediate the connection between what is known and what is sought by drawing the image of the soul on the skin.

Right: This glowing-faced bartender wears whimsical tattoos that display his love of music.

Below: Sax player, Jeremy Carter, says his tattoos, which include musical, mystical, and family images, are a "work in progress."

Above: A seeing eye tattoo offers protection for this young woman.

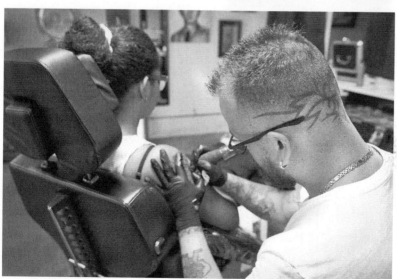

With loving hands and heart, this tattoo artist begins applying her niece's first tattoo—a bouquet of flowers.

Chapter 8: The Language of Recovery

Sometimes you can only find Heaven by slowly backing away from Hell. —Carrie Fisher

*This woman's cheerful smile and happy tropical tattoos
bring comfort to those who've "been through it."*

I have to admit that I am one of *those* guys—I am in love with my truck. My 1998 Toyota Land Cruiser is like a 98-year-old man who wants to live but won't give up three packs of cigarettes a day. At 440,000 miles, I've got the equivalent of almost 18 trips around the world at on it, and it's still going. My dog, my truck, and I have been to Canada, the Florida Keys, the Midwest, and all points in between. Will I be buried in it? Of course I will! What kind of question is that?

Recently, first gear went out. I was at Assateague Beach and a log tore through the transmission line. There's always something. Now when my truck breaks, it needs me and I'm there to nurse it back to health. My mechanic says, "You know, it's okay to hang out here while we work on your truck; we understand separation anxiety, Mr. Dayhoff." I didn't know it was that obvious.

Some of the miles I've put on my four-wheeled companion have been eaten up visiting junkyards. After all, the junkyard is where old cars go to die—but not before their organs are harvested and bones are picked over. Why spend a fortune for a new part when you can strip one off an old workhorse for half the price? Every part in good working order breathes new life into my baby.

But even though these places are called "junkyards," don't let the name fool you—there's staggering value in the parts and sheet metal. And that's why these places are guarded by the infamous junkyard dog, the meaner and nastier the better.

No ordinary dog is fit for duty at the junkyard. As a dog lover, it pains me to know that dogs who do this work are trained to attack intruders with unequaled ferocity. They cannot be domesticated, otherwise they would lose their wild edge. They have minimal human contact, so the bond dogs crave will not be formed. They're fed just enough to keep them healthy but are always left hungry. The deprivation a junkyard dog experiences creates a twitchy, edgy menace that will scare the living daylights out of anyone. Here's the thing, though. The dog is just doing what he has been trained to do when anyone gets too close. It's the junkyard owner who values his property.

I'm thinking of one dog who guards a yard in southern Maryland. A Doberman cross, he's got one torn eye socket and long half-healed scars on his back, maybe from chasing intruders under junk cars. At the close of business, the high stockade gates are closed and he's let loose to wander inside the property. His job is to attack anyone or anything that enters his domain. He's fast and loud, and his bark is as bad as his bite.

Though we aren't always conscious of it, everyone has junk in their soul, stuff that we're not quite sure what to do with. it's what we've inherited from the complicated family dynamics and personal experiences that make us who we are. It might be worth something, but it's so much work to wade through the years of piled-up experiences that we're not sure we could extract anything valuable from even if we found it. And what happens if you pull out the wrong things? Then what?

No matter what we think or feel about this mixed bag of hand-me-downs, it's ours. Some of it is real, honest-to-goodness junk, and some of it is the unpolished jewels that are the essence of our lives. Now, along with the junk and jewels, some of us have a junkyard dog, prowling around to keep away anyone who comes near.

So what is this junkyard dog and what is he guarding? Maybe it's our anxiety about ourselves that makes us a little crazy. Maybe it's our despair or depression. Maybe it's the aftereffects from a life-altering struggle, like a meth addiction. Maybe it's an unhealed wound that has stolen years of peace and safety from your heart, like a father's cruel, dignity-piercing words you've heard for years, even after he's gone.

Sometimes our junkyard dog is hypervigilant, lurking just one or two thoughts away. For many of us, it's not whether the dog will be tamed—though we've tried to before—but how we deal with the threat of an attack, because he's there, always there, guarding the owner's stuff.

In my experience, tattoos often tell the story of a junkyard dog who lives behind the gate of the soul, where our stuff is. As I watch and listen to people, I have to wonder if the tattoo is there to force its owner to deal with the growling dog.

What's your junkyard dog?

A vendetta

I met Anthony at the junkyard when I was looking for a power-steering pump for my truck. His thick, greasy hair and his Fonzie-like attitude seemed a perfect fit for his work. My guess is he was a cousin to the junkyard dog. I handed him the paper that said I had paid for a part. I needed Anthony to scour the junkyard for the organ donor: a half-dead Land Cruiser.

"Can I come along?" I asked.

"Not allowed," he responded.

"Please?"

"Okay, mister. But don't tell the boss."

He was economical with his words; he used eye glances and nods. We walked around a lot of dead cars before spotting a 1998 Land Cruiser just like mine, except it was green, and had no shoes, glasses, or seats. But I could still see her original beauty. I watched eagerly as Anthony worked to unbolt the precious hydraulic pump that would give new life to my truck back home.

"Nice tattoos, I remarked," referring to his whole arm that strained to free the pump.

No response.

"I bet that took a while."

No response.

"I'm guessing it cost a lot of money to have all those done."

Not even an acknowledgment of my presence, let alone that I said anything. Then, after a long pause Anthony spoke.

"I left my gang in Colombia," he said in a thick accent. "They killed my little brother."

I looked closer at his arm. I saw pictures of two little boys playing, a cross, tears; the Madonna, and a mother figure. Then I saw the unmistakable symbols of war—guns, knives, and rope.

"When I make enough money, I'm going back to get even. It's gonna happen."

"I'm sorry, my friend."

"I wish I could stop hating but can't. Only when I think of my family in heaven does it stop."

After that Anthony was out of words. He blinked and nodded at me, which perhaps meant "thanks." His junkyard dog is revenge.

Milestones

For some people I interviewed, the junkyard dog's bark was echoed in tattoos of tears, blood, revenge, burning flesh, tombstones, or a middle finger. For others, the tattoo was a lid on a pressure cooker, or even a well-disguised portal to a soul's desperate prayer for peace and recovery. Tattoos also tell about the recovery process, the heat of the battle, and wars won and lost. In fact, the skin of some tattoo owners has become a like a war college, a place where the enemy's strategies can be studied.

Many people in substance-abuse recovery wear tattoos. It seems like the soul needs to document its journey back to health. After being sober for 18 months, one young woman celebrated her recovery with a tattoo—a rising sun. It spoke to me of a new day. When she's been sober for 24 months, she'll get another one. Her tattoos will become journal entries, recording her sobriety milestones.

Many tattoos mark newfound peace or healing. Some wear images that inspire strength, hope, and courage to persevere in the effort to be whole again, one day at a time. I've seen other folks in recovery who use powerful words and phrases, inked in ornate calligraphy, that speak to their junkyard dog—*Dedicated*—*One day at a time*—*I Believe*—*Faith*—and Bible verses that speak of a God who fights steadfastly for them.

Deliverance

I was in line at a Starbucks and Karen, 27-ish, was two people ahead of me. I was trying not to stare; her young skin was covered in beautiful poetry. She ordered a grande white chocolate mocha and luckily turned to walk past me.

I caught her eye with a smile. "Hi! Love your tattoos. Got a second for a few honest questions?"

I could immediately tell that her creepy-guy antennae went up, but she warily consented. My drink was in a ceramic mug, which signaled that I was there for more than a quick coffee. I pointed to a hard chair and she sat down. She leaned away from me, holding her cup with both hands, her body facing the door.

"I'm learning about tattoos, so I can write about them," I explained.

"I don't see any on *you*," she replied, outing me as a potential imposter.

"I guess I'm afraid of the pain, and I don't want to cry in front of some tattoo guy."

She relaxed at my funny admission.

"Do you have a story on your arm?" I asked.

The orientation of tattooed writing often reveals the owner's intention. The first orientation lets it be read most easily by the person who wears it; the second points outward for observers to read; and a third is hidden so no one can read it. There are also "peekaboo" tattoos, curious half-revealed pictures or words that give you only a part of the story. Some owners intend this as a tease. In Karen's case, the script of her tattoo was placed so that she could read it, but I could not.

She told me that the words came from the Bible, but she didn't know where or if they were really there. She valued this message— enough to pay $880 to have it permanently written on her skin. The words were in pretty cursive on the inside of her forearm, facing her.

She read the words to me: "Because the Lord your God is in the midst of you, and will fight for you against your enemies, to deliver you from danger and your enemies."

I asked, "Who's the enemy God is fighting for you?"

She paused, narrowed her eyes with a flash of emotion and looked away. Only then did I notice that one side of her body was a little different, sort of sagging.

"I had a stroke when I was 15 and lost control of the right side of my body. It used to be really bad. I was teased a lot by other kids. I stopped going out in public and just sort of hid for a number of years. After I went to therapy it got better. I can walk and talk much better now." She paused, "You really want to hear this?" she asked.

"I do, honey. I feel like you're letting me join you on a sacred journey. Thank you."

"The words talk about coming to a place where all you've got left is the hope that someone else will pick up the battle. I find comfort in the idea that God will fight for me. But I'm not always sure it's true. I wish it was true."

"You gave me more than I bargained for, friend."

"Will I be in your book? I sure hope so." She got up and threw me a squinty smile. "Goodbye," she said, and was gone. I went home to look up the words of her tattoo. They are in the Old Testament, Deuteronomy 20:4

For the Lord your God is the one who goes with you to fight for you against your enemies to give you victory.

Sometimes, tattoos tell the story of the journey of recovery. This was one of those times.

Letting it out

Anyone who's ever attended an Alcoholics Anonymous meeting knows that "recovery" is what we call the process of recognizing that something is wrong and saying it out loud to someone else. Similarly, tattoos often say out loud what the soul recognizes about the mixed bag of junk that lies inside. The ones I've seen illustrate a journey inspired by hope.

A tattoo can symbolize a journey of recovery from sexual abuse, drug addiction, or deep emotional wounds of abuse or abandonment. A tattoo can highlight recovery milestones, like celebrating 20 years being clean from cocaine. It can signal the battle plan to win recovery one step or one day at a time. It can also be a cry for recovery one day in the future, because right now the junkyard dog is terribly fierce.

The boy who loved trains

I met Johnson outside a McDonald's in Washington, DC. It was around 11:30 P.M., and he was in a blanket lying on the sidewalk about 10 feet from the door. I'm a health food junkie, except when I'm not. When I'm not, watch out! I was heading inside for two cheeseburgers, small fries, and an Oreo McFlurry. Heaven, baby!

But I saw this guy, and he had tattoos, and I had to know more. He glanced at me when I walked in.

When I ordered, I asked for four cheeseburgers, two small fries, and two McFlurries. I hoped that if I shared my food, Johnson might be willing to share his secrets. I had the cashier put the contents in two separate bags. I walked out and handed one to Johnson.

He perked up and took the bag. "Thank you very much, sir, and God bless you."

I sensed that he might not have been mentally stable, so I was careful, not wanting to make him angry or steal his few moments of dignity while he ate a late-night meal.

"There's no salt in here!" he said, raising his voice loudly.

"I'll get some," I said.

I went back inside and returned to Johnson with those little packets that lose most of the salt when you tear them open. It didn't seem wise to sit on the ground, so I bent down into a squat about three feet away from him.

"I'm a McDonald's cheeseburger addict." I offered.

"Addictions can kill you," he said authoritatively.

"I like your tattoos."

He bristled, "So you think they're stupid?"

"No, in fact I'm guessing they probably have a good story behind them. Do you like stories?" I asked.

"Yeah, and my name is Johnson. Just Johnson. Not Joe Johnson. Just ... Johnson!"

"Johnson, do your tattoos have a story?"

No reply. He kept eating. He didn't answer for about five long minutes. I wasn't sure if I should stay or not. But, usually the longer I wait, the more likely it is that something big is just on the other side of the silence.

Finally, Johnson pulled the blanket away to show me a tattoo of a train. He was dirty and unshaven, maybe in his sixties, and had only a few teeth left.

"Like my train?"

"I love trains."

"If you wait long enough, one will come by, and you can hear it pass."

He looked down at his tattoo and said, "I once had a little boy, he loved trains because I loved trains. I haven't seen him and don't know where he is."

I didn't want to steal anything from this moment by asking deep questions, but I did ask one more.

"Johnson, I have one question. When the train comes, and you hear it, or feel it from the ground, does it make you feel better?"

"How did you know that?" he asked.

And just then, honest to God, we heard a late-night train rumbling in the distance.

The chrysalis

I was visiting a friend at Johns Hopkins Hospital in Baltimore, Maryland. My visit coincided with the nurse's arrival to change the bedding and check on medication drips, so I was asked to take a break in the waiting room down the hall. I found a *Hot Rod* magazine and started looking at pictures of ridiculous muscle cars that I can remember drooling over when I was a kid in high school.

After a few minutes, a woman in her late thirties came in and sat down next to me. I leaned away, a little embarrassed by my boyish choice of magazine. I pondered exchanging it for one on science, but a tiny conversation was born before I could get up.

"Hello," she said.

"Hi, my name is Al. And you?"

"Shirley."

I'm still not sure why the next words came out of my mouth, "So, come here a lot?" Before I even finished the sentence I felt even dumber than I had about the magazine.

"Yes, I get chemo here every week."

Then I noticed the pretty scarf covering her hairless head and a tube that probably led to her port for treatment. I guess my expression told her how foolish I felt.

"It's OK," she said. "But the radiation and chemo can make you pretty sick. I can't do the anti-nausea meds because they make things worse."

"I'm so sorry."

Now that I had finally gotten past my own self-consciousness, I noticed her tattoos—a swarm of butterflies. They were different sizes and colors and seemed to be flying from her back around to the front of her chest.

"I like your tattoos."

She said, "It was probably wasn't smart to do chemo and tattoos at the same time, but it seemed like a good idea."

"What do you mean?"

"Well, I have young children and we all believe that butterflies bring miracles, like a caterpillar becomes a butterfly."

Once again, words fell out of my mouth before I could catch them, "So do you feel like a caterpillar now?"

"She laughed and blushed, "You know, I think so. But I'm on my way to being a butterfly and that's what I tell my three kids."

I realized that I was still in a hot rod brain looking at a beautiful woman that just wanted to have a real connection.

When she blinked it was as if she had pulled up a shade that let me see inside. She told me she had Stage 4 breast cancer and felt scared. I sat in silence as I listened.

"You are beautiful already, my friend, and I believe God is watching over you and your children. I will pray for your healing, if that's okay."

When her name was called, I reached over and patted her hand. As she got up and left with the nurse, I watched Shirley's butterflies fly with her.

Recovery

Tattoos tell the story the junkyard within, and the dog who guards it. They also express the progressive steps of recovery. Shirley was likely scared of dying. But she seemed even more sensitive to the pain that her disease is causing in the tender hearts of her young children. Getting tattooed at the same time she's being treated for cancer is like heaping insult on top of injury. But I could see the wisdom in it. Shirley wanted butterflies to give her children, and herself, some peace and hope for recovery.

Many people don't realize that tattoos document internal battles, difficult steps in recovery, or a space in the soul between those two delicate places. I've been deeply moved by how intimate and personal a person's tattoos are, and even more by the welcome I've received from their owners as I glimpse their true meaning. It's a rare thing to be invited to see into a person's fragile soul. But it's also unnerving, humbling. Why? Because when someone opens the door to the most intimate, most sacred place of their lives, I cannot enter without metaphorically taking off my shoes. In fact, I have to take off whatever self-preoccupation I have—the mask, and the public persona—to be vulnerable to what someone wants to show me. Sometimes I suddenly realize that both of us are stripped of the pretensions that keep us at arm's length from others.

In this kind of exchange there's no way for me to connect without becoming keenly aware that there's a pile of junk stacked up in my soul, too, and it's not all pretty. Real communion between two souls just does that to you.

If you think tattoos are just about a bunch of lost people who can't get a job or want to be viewed as a bad-to-the-bone outcast, you're wrong. And, if you think your own personal junkyard dog has been tamed, well, I'd challenge you to think again. Maybe it's time for a tattoo, eh? It could just start talking to you about what's really real on the inside.

Above and left: This young natural wellness educator, explains that she's been "healed by the grace of God," and has a tattoo that reads, "All good things are wild & free."

About her tattoos she says, "I came from a life of chronic horrible pain and partial temporary paralysis episodes in my legs to discovering natural wellness and living life to the fullest. So it seemed fitting!"

This young woman's tattoos
plead for understanding.

Below: This woman's first tattoo was done to cover up scars on her arm from a bite this very dog once gave her.

Chapter 9: It's Not Just Your Skin Talking

The wearer of this tattoo says that, "It's the sacred geometry of the hemp plant. It's known by the Japanese name Asanoha. It represents the microcosm (geometry) that makes up the macrocosm (in this case the physical hemp plant), and quotes Hermes Trismegistus, "As above, so below, as within, so without, as the universe, so the soul...."

As I write this chapter, I sense I'm walking in a tension, but a tension I welcome. I'm an ordained Presbyterian minister and have loved and embraced my calling to share and nourish faith in the beautiful souls who come across my path. For some reason, thousands of very non-church people have come into my life. This has been an unexpected gift that gives me so much joy. I have learned so much about myself, about life, and about God from them.

One thing I have learned is that Life is a journey of faith that leads to surprising discoveries. Many of the people I've met ask profound spiritual questions, like: "If God is real, if God is so great, why is there so much suffering?" Often they ask these questions through their tattoos. For reasons that may or may not be apparent, profound spiritual questions asked through tattoos don't fit easily into the organized church community. They might not fit well in any religious institution, although I think they should. If you can't ask questions there, where can you? But they do fit well in the wild, in the public space.

I'd like to ask both groups of my friends, in and out of the church, to consider what I'm about to say.

First, my dear church friends, I want you to consider this: The idea that God could be revealed in fullness through flesh and blood—something you take for granted—was once considered the ultimate heresy! Remember how the religious leaders in Jesus' day berated Him when he claimed, "If you have seen me you have seen the Father," and "I and my Father are one?" That's what sealed his fate on the cross! In its time, nothing could have been more repulsive to the spiritual and theological sensibilities of the faithful.

Now I'm going to posit something else for you to consider: the idea that God used the skin of his Son to communicate with us. I understand that for many faithful Christians, this idea might be abhorrent. And yet that seems to be exactly what has happened in the body of Jesus, both at the time of his resurrection and at the time of his promised return.

We know that Jesus' disciples were moved to reverent belief not only because he visibly appeared to them—alive after death. It was seeing and, for some, *touching* the marks in his hands, his side, and his feet that convinced them. But the marks on Jesus' body communicate a message that doesn't end there. According to Revelation 19:16, when He returns to the world in glory it will be with a message etched "[o]n His robe <u>and on His thigh</u> He has this name written: King of kings and

Lord of lords." God has tattooed Jesus with a message intended to be seen.

Though it argues with our sensibilities, it seems to me that God uses images on human skin, even the skin of Christ Himself, as a way to tell us what He wants us to know.

And to you, my dear friends outside of the church: Your willingness to ask questions that challenge my faith gets me out of bed every day. Because you let me listen to you, we have forged a love out of authentic disclosure and respect. Thank you for allowing me in, under, and around your tattoo. I marvel at your introspection as you make discoveries about what's in your soul, tethered to your tattoos. You have allowed me to watch and quietly ask what is happening in your life.

Morse code

Samuel Morse was born in 1791. He graduated from Yale in 1810 and began his career as an artist. But his creativity could not be restricted, and he began to tinker with telegraphy, sending electrical impulses over wires. Morse vastly improved existing telegraphy it by combining a multiple-wire system into a single-wire process. In 1837 he patented the electromagnetic telegraph, and later helped create an eponymous system that could send complex messages using electrical signals coded as dots and dashes. It wasn't long before the United States had telegraph poles running across the country; Europe also adopted the Morse system as its standard.

Beginning In the 1850s, warfare was forever changed when battlefield communications times collapsed from hours to seconds. Telegraphy played a prominent role during the American Civil War, and it changed the strategies and outcome of both World Wars. Morse's invention laid the groundwork for future inventions that include the telephone, radio, television, and internet. But even in the modern era Morse code remained useful.

One heart-stopping incident from the Vietnam War concerns naval aviator Jeremiah Denton, who was held as a prisoner of war in North Vietnam for almost eight years after his plane was shot down during a bombing mission. In 1966 Denton's captors forced him to participate in a televised press conference. While answering questions about the conditions of his captivity, he pretended to have light sensitivity that caused his eyes to blink in an irregular manner. But he was actually using Morse code to spell out the word T-O-R-T-U-R-E. This message confirmed to US Naval Intelligence what had been long suspected about the treatment of American POWs. Denton spent four more years in solitary confinement, including two years in a windowless 3-by-9-foot cell, mostly in irons. When he was finally freed in 1973 he revealed that his torture had increased following the interview.

Today, we live in a world where instant communication links different parts of the world. But there is another kind of messaging, a spiritual communication, that does not depend on cutting-edge technology. God speaks to us through the skin of His Son Jesus. And many people, knowingly or not, speak back to God by inking messages on the their skin.

Some, especially those in the church community, view tattoos as a mutilation of the body and a sign of disrespect for God. But in my experience, as I have interviewed and listened to people, their tattoos seem like messages *to* God—messages that ask for His help, forgiveness, and love. I'm coming to believe that some tattoos are like a spiritual Morse code being used by the human soul to communicate with God.

I'm not defending tattoos. They need no defense. I know what I've experienced and what I've seen. Tattoos are a significant way that people express themselves; they seem to help them access the deepest reaches of their soul to send messages that cannot be fully expressed in any other way. Can you see them? Can you hear them? Millions of souls are sending messages to speak their *sighs too deep for words.* (Romans 8:26)

Jeremiah Denton was desperate to tell the truth about his captivity. That desperation drove him to ingeniously adapt Morse code—in the blink of an eye—to send his critically important message.

Could it be that the image of God in each soul has become so desperate to be heard that it is now writing on the live canvas of the skin? If so, how can we read or hear the language of tattoos if we don't have the key to unlock their messages? Once I thought there must be some cryptic, secret knowledge that was the key. So I just started talking to people, asking questions, and listening to what they wanted to say. The more I did this the more I awakened to the discovery that the key is love—love expressed in empathy.

Empathy

The only way I can be the recipient of deeply personal life stories, often filled with breathtaking vulnerability, is through empathy—that is, to be present with respect, honesty, patience, and curiosity. A lot of the time, the greater beneficiary of this exchange is the person who does the disclosing.

The expression of empathy is not simply a clever device I use to get people to open up. Having true empathy means opening yourself to the experience by making yourself vulnerable to the very same questions, doubts, fears, anxieties, and suffering. Our English word "empathy" comes from two Greek words that combine to mean "in passion" or "in feeling." Empathy is the ability to have a heart for, and to *enter into* the circumstances and situations that someone else has lived.

Empathy isn't simply saying "Oh, I'm sorry," when we hear about misfortune or pain. It is experiencing that sorrow, identifying with it and the person conveying it, often via body language and facial expressions. That's why a light touch of the hand, a tear, a knowing look, or a hug can be healing medicine for a vulnerable soul.

We all use words. But words are not what people respond to. It's how I am with them. When you feel that someone is really with you, not just in the space near you, then you have the sense that they understand you—they *see* you. And when people *see* us, we feel safe and can risk opening up to reveal deeper, more real, essential parts of ourselves: the parts that matter most.

But some of us are so uncomfortable with what is really going on in our own lives that the last thing we want is to be vulnerable to someone else's struggle. So when someone is desperate to be noticed in their pain, pain that we can't handle, we'll pretend to have empathy by only speaking the words. Never in a million years would we want to risk feeling the passion or suffering that is roiling inside, because we fear we might be consumed by it.

I'm coming to believe that we are so afraid of being eaten alive by life's experiences that, though we have not chosen to live as hermits, we might as well have. Even though we still participate in life with our families and communities, some of us have erected shells that protect us from dangerous exposure to the mess in someone else's life. It also lets us hide the junk we keep secret from everyone else.

Where tattoos take us

When I've asked, "Why did you get that tattoo?" a number of people answered, "It made me feel better." I suspect this has to do with a deep longing for empathy. They chose a tattoo as a way to name a person, place, thing, or experience that is deeply, fundamentally important to them. It could be something that needed recognition or validation, something that longed for understanding and support, or something (or someone) they were grieving. A tattoo floats like a buoy on the surface, but is tethered to an anchor deep below. It can be a starting point for the person who wants to find the way into his own soul. Diving to reach the experience, he is guided by the tether that connects the soul to his outer life.

More than ever, ours seems to be a time when souls feel compelled to write on their skin. Why? Because people feel disconnected. Think of it: Studies show that even with the explosion of technology that promises instant connectedness, people are more isolated and lonely than ever. We're taking and posting selfies all over the internet. "See me!" they seem to cry. Everything is photographed—what we ate for breakfast, a new pair of shoes—the list is endless. Yet even though we seem driven to chronicle the details of our lives, selfies can't delve into the recesses of our souls where, it seems, we may really want to go. It's as if we're clamoring to be seen as we really are, but are stuck, trapped inside a realm that we can't break out of.

In 1988 a genius collaboration between Disney Studios and Stephen Spielberg's Amblin Entertainment produced the hugely successful movie *Who Framed Roger Rabbit?* Its groundbreaking technology combined film photography with hand-drawn cartoon characters—without the benefit of computer animation. Theaters were packed with audiences of all ages who couldn't wait to see this amazing cinematography that integrated two worlds. Two-dimensional characters had broken into the three-dimensional world of living people.

Right now it feels like three-dimensional people are trying to break into the fourth dimension—the realm of the spirit—but haven't found the way to do it. I suspect the way has always been there; we've just lost it and are desperately trying to find it again. In the meantime, whether it's by digital technology or old-fashioned needle and ink on a living canvas, people are expressing their desperation to pierce the veil of the ordinary in search of a dimension to which they are increasingly drawn. People wearing tattoos are saying, "Here is my journal. This is who I am. This is where I come from. This is what I am discovering. This is my story and I want to be known, to myself, to you, and to the One who is in, under, by, around, and through all of it."

I see this trend popping up in the religious community, which is also getting more tattoos. In many churches tattoos can be seen everywhere. In my research, a very large percentage of the tattoos I've seen include religious images—the face of Jesus, pictures representing His resurrection, Bible verses, rosaries, angel's wings, the Virgin Mary, and words like forgiveness, love, mercy and grace written in pictures and poems. One minister told me that he wanted "to be one of them, be among them, and delight in the tattoo culture." Another pastor asked, "So many tattoos are about loss, pain, confusion, change, and tears. Is there any room for praise, hope, prayers, joy, and pictures of heaven?"

I think this question is telling, and it comes from a lot of folks—not just the religious. Some people see tattoo images as wounds, hurts to be healed, problems to be fixed. We are so obsessed with fixing things! We want to do away with ambiguity that provokes discomfort. But what if these images are both at the same time—signs of a wound, the hope for recovery, and the recovery itself?

According to Christianity, hope is not in Jesus as God, but in Jesus as God who lived and suffered as a man. The triumph of Easter is empty without the soul-wrenching, life-ending drama of Good Friday's crucifixion. Hope, prayers, praise and joy don't just hang in midair by themselves. They are a response to life-threatening, soul-shattering events that are as much a part of life as the air we breathe.

I confess that though I don't wear a tattoo to illustrate it, it is my appreciation for the pathos, the journey of a person who lives through suffering, that touches me almost more deeply than anything else. I feel a depth of reality in this dichotomy between good and evil that makes me shake my head in awe for what people live through. It makes my heart ache for the sheer mercy and grace that must undergird the souls who mark their journey on their skin, like a testament that says, "Though I am here now, this is where I have been."

I've said that this book rose out of my curiosity about why people are writing on themselves. Then, in the middle of my research I wondered, did God write on Jesus? In the gospel story of His passion, His skin had profound significance for those who believe.

The needle-pointed thorns of the mocking crown cut His brow. He was scourged with a whip whose barbell-shaped pieces of metal were designed to strip away the flesh. The scriptures say, "By His stripes (the marks left by the scourge on his body) we are healed." As He hung on the cross—the Romans' preferred method of execution—His body was brutally attached to the wood with nails that pierced His hands and feet. His side was pierced with a spear. Something about the suffering inflicted on Him, attested to by the marks on His body, has redemptive value for our soul.

Raging bull

I met Gary in a Walmart, in the camping supplies aisle. I was buying propane tanks for my truck and getting ready for a trip to West Virginia. He seemed like a good old boy, very large, and decked out in worn camouflage hunting clothes. He was muscular, damned muscular. His tattoos would move when he flexed or twitched. I couldn't decide what his flexing movement was about, what was causing it.

I know you won't be surprised to learn that curiosity got the best of me. I had to find out about his tattoos. I hoped there would be witnesses in case I fumbled my approach. I really didn't want to trigger anything bad, especially his anger.

Do you remember that scene in the *Wizard of Oz* where Dorothy, the Lion, the Scarecrow, and the Tin Man stood in front of the giant flaming image of Oz, the great and powerful, who spoke with smoke and fire? Oz's real name could have been Gary. Gary had a big, angry looking tattoo all the way down his arm. It was a charging, angry demon, like a bull, snorting fire and trampling over bones. They looked like human bones.

Tentatively, but telling myself I had the confidence to do this, I said, "I like your tattoos, man. They seem to have a message."

Sure enough, the demon-like bull appeared in Gary's expression. I backed up and started talking fast.

"I ... I'm doing research and need a few people to help me out. I'm not very good at asking about these things."

Gary looked away and resumed his shopping. But then he spoke. "Life's a bitch, right? Anything you do, it can and will go wrong. Right?"

How many times I've heard that question!

"My name is Al, by the way."

Still a little wary, I reached out my hand. His thick, hard skin engulfed my wimpy paw.

I forged ahead. "Can I ask what the bull is?

Bull's-eye!

"IT'S WHOEVER THE BASTARD IS WHO'S IN CHARGE OF THIS S***HOLE!"

"You mean God?" I said.

"If that's what you want to call him, up to you."

"So the bull is God?"

"Yeah."

"What's that he's running over on your arm? I don't understand."

"God's a bully. He sets you up, teases you with things like a job, a girlfriend, or a kid … and then just steals them away. I hope it makes the bastard happy."

"I'm sorry friend."

"Yeah, me too."

And he was gone. Not only did he have an angry tattoo, an angry face, and an angry voice, his exit was angry too. I pondered his words as he disappeared down the aisle and rounded the corner. It looked to me like the intended recipient of Gary's message was God Himself. Like Jeremiah Denton, Gary was signaling his torture from losses that were unbearably painful.

I thought of the axiom, "The louder the anger, the deeper the hurt." But even when the anger is directed at Him, I think God can take it. In fact, He wants to hear it. In God's creative, counterintuitive way, the wound is exactly what He wants to know. Often the raging protest turns into introspection. And when the heart is finally vulnerable, the pain that fueled the rage can be healed. He is the Great Physician of the soul, but it often takes time before His treatment can be received.

I find that even if the tattoo's message is angry and defiant toward God, it's still talking to Him. It's like when my kids were teenagers and I suddenly found myself in the season called dad-is-a-complete-and-utter-idiot. I found it was important during those times to keep the conversation going, even if it was laced with disrespect, blaming, and a ton of misunderstanding.

God can take it, and my guess is He may well be connecting with Gary's soul through that angry bull tattoo. God gets it. He can decipher the code, and he does.

When I hear torment like Gary's, I can't help but hear the words of Jesus on the cross. He was scarred, body and soul, by the worst life can dish out. In the midst of this torture he cried, "My God, my God, why have you forsaken me?" (Matthew 27:46) Gary's tattoo was also screaming his pain at God. His rage cried out, "How could you treat me like this? If You are there, why can't You save me from the pain that comes from just being human on this planet?"

Getting a tattoo breaks the skin; it hurts. When the needle pierces the skin, the customer winces because he feels the pain right there, in his skin. Some inkers love it, some hate it, but they all describe a high that comes from the pain: Something magical happens. Science can explain it in medical and biological terms, but it's still magical. The tattoo wound heals. Like a little child who falls and scrapes his knee, his mind fixes on the pain of the body's torn wrapper. But then the skin heals. Whether a fall leaves a scar or the tattoo needle leaves an image, in the end there is healing, and a sign of what happened is left behind.

The world is full of grace

Jessie was standing by the river watching her dog swim. I'd just pulled up to the landing so mine could do the same thing. I walked around the back of my truck and released my 115-pound swim-crazed chocolate Lab. He was terribly excited and sprinted toward Jessie's yellow Lab before I could stop him.

"Oh, sorry," I yelled, hoping a fight wouldn't break out. "Harley is all run and no bite," I tried to reassure her.

They sniffed each other like dogs do, a whole different form of skin communication. I walked up to the water's edge with the ball. Soon Harley forgot all about his new friend and was ready for a good game of aquatic catch. I pitched the solid rubber ball as hard as I could. It landed about three hundred feet out into the fast river. Before it left my hand, Harley was in pursuit, bounding into the water.

"Is he going to come back?" the lady asked.

"Yeah, just watch."

Keeping one eye on Harley, I looked over and saw that Jessie had a tattoo that appeared to cover her whole back. I wondered what she was saying with it.

"I like your tattoo," I said.

"Thanks. Just got it."

"Still hurt?" I asked.

"No. It's all healed."

"So may I ask what it means?"

"Well, my daughter was diagnosed with leukemia, and it changed the whole way I was living and thinking. My mom and I went to war against it with her diet, and drugs, and all those damned doctor appointments. I think she missed a year of school."

"By the way, my name is Al, and yours?"

"Jessie, and my daughter's Grace."

"Please tell me more, Jessie."

"Well, I'm not a church person or anything, and don't have anything against God since He's never really been mean to me, but … this time it was different."

"What do you mean?"

"We couldn't stop the leukemia, it just kept stealing her life. One night I walked around the hospital crying. I couldn't stop. I just cried, and cried, asking God why was He doing this to Grace! I promised Him I'd be better, and stop smoking, and cussing, and be nicer to my ex, and … whatever He wanted if He could just heal my daughter! Then it happened. She just got better! It changed me so much that I wrote a big old tattoo on my back."

"Can I see it?"

"Sure you can."

She lifted her shirt. All across her back was a picture of the world—the sun, moon, and sky; the forest; animals and birds; and in the middle was a mom holding her little girl in one hand and waving upward with the other.

Just then Harley pulled himself out of the river, ran up next to us, and shook water all over Jessie. She laughed.

"I've got to go. Grace's bus comes in 15 minutes."

I thanked her. She smiled, and seemed overwhelmed with emotion, like a cry could come any second. And then she turned and walked away.

Five questions

In my research I've bumped into something: Everybody has thoughts about who they are, where they came from, and why. Sometimes they just have questions. But most of the time they have a

154

pretty good idea of what they think about these things. I've found that when I ask five specific questions the floodgates open. Out pours a lifetime of experience, analysis, struggle, pain, and hope. Mind you, I don't always ask the questions in quite the formal way you're about to read them. Often, the questions are implied by what people say in the course of telling their story. I try not to add anything to the conversation, just reflect back to people what I hear them say, or what I hear them signaling. Almost always, what they say to me refines what they really believe.

Taking people as they are, right where they are, is a powerful thing. As I say, it releases a torrent of disclosure about what really matters in the depth of a person's soul. Tattoo conversations are particularly amazing because the person has already gone to the trouble of working over something that is deep inside, something that is essential about who they are. So here are the questions and a sampling of what some people think about them.

Where do you believe the world came from? One man had tattoos of various transitions from monkey to human that finally morphed into a monkey-man who seemed to resemble himself. I guess he was saying he believed in evolution, and perhaps that he was still evolving. Then there was Jeff, with a tattoo of a spaceship landing to populate the earth—with beer and Amazon women. I'd need to ask him a few more questions to know what he really meant.

What do you believe about God? Many people are angry with God or confused about His disappearing acts, and what they believe is His skewed sense of justice. One man had a tattoo of God asleep on a throne. Another had the Mother Mary with her arms around a group of little children.

What do you believe about Jesus? A lot of people choose cross tattoos. I've seen them in every shape, style, and design. One man had the nail holes inked into his palms that looked as if they went right through to the back of his hand. I've met more agnostics with crosses than I can count. Perhaps the soul is saying, "If you tattoo a cross, He will show up."

What do you believe about life after death? There are tattoos that have a profound sense of mortality, the limit of our minutes on earth, and loss that can happen any moment. I saw this expressed in a tattoo worn by a lady in line at a Starbucks: "Let the good times roll, because when you're dead, you're done! Party on!"

If you could ask God one question what would it be? I think this question generates most of the messages that are conveyed through tattoos. But while tattoos ask questions, they also collect information like a huge NASA space dish. How do I know? I've spent thousands of hours of listening to the layers of meaning that people have acquired over the period of time they've lived with their tattoos. Remember, a tattoo may look like one thing. But for a lot of people, its meaning is constantly morphing as they realize new insights.

If you talk with someone about their tattoo, I'm willing to bet that almost everything you will hear will either be an answer to one of these questions, or an expansion of it. Tattoos signal what our soul believes, or wants to believe, about life.

What could have been

Kim was sitting on a bench in Virginia Beach, Virginia, maybe waiting for a bus, or maybe just waiting. I had coffee in my cup and decided to enjoy it by sitting down next to her. Yup, she had a number of tattoos. They were pretty and colorful. I didn't sit close but did say hello and casually started a conversation.

"I like your tattoos. May I ask what that one means?"

The tattoo I pointed to was a little girl with bare feet and a pretty, wispy dress. You could tell she was little-girl happy, playful, and just being what three year olds should be. Kim paused and looked at the ground. I waited, realizing that I might be entering a sacred space in her soul. She couldn't have been more than 24, but she had the wise eyes of someone well-travelled.

"It's a little girl who would have been about four right now."

"She's pretty. Is she your little girl?"

"Yeah, she is."

Another long pause, maybe the all-time-longest pause of my tattoo research. For a few seconds I thought "She's so lost in her thought she might have forgotten I'm here." Or was she ignoring me? Waiting usually lets me know.

"Yeah, she's in heaven."

"Oh, I'm sorry."

"Well, me and her dad, we just got pregnant. And he left. And well, I went to the clinic, and that was that." She got silent, but then, "I'm not a bad person."

"Of course you're not, honey, God bless you. Does she have a name?"

She looked at me and said, I named her Bumble Bee. I'm hoping she is in heaven waiting for me. It might be a long time before I can see her."

"Very sweet," I said.

The bus came, and Kim smiled and waved to me as she boarded. Later that day I saw a bee and thought of the pretty young woman on the bench and the little girl waiting for her in heaven.

God marked Cain

The Bible says God tattooed someone. It's in the first book of the Bible, Genesis, which tells the story of Cain, who killed his brother Abel.

The Lord said, "What have you done? ... Now you are under a curse and driven from the ground. ... When you work the ground, it will no longer yield its crops for you. You will be a restless wanderer on the earth.
Cain said to the Lord, "My punishment is more than I can bear. ... I will be hidden from your presence; I will be a restless wanderer on the earth, and whoever finds me will kill me."
Then the Lord put a mark on Cain so that no one who found him would kill him. (Genesis 4:10–15)

Many people wonder what this mark could have been. Was it the first tattoo? Did it tell the story of loss and pain, or did it symbolize his curse? Whatever it was, it was clearly visible to other people, and whatever it said, those who might try to harm Cain were warned not to.

Notice it says, "no one who found him." Not everyone who saw Cain was necessarily able to understand that his mark had a meaning. But "those who found him" did. When you engage someone because of their tattoo, are you on the verge of finding them, finding the real person? And when a tattooed person is "found," should you respect them as having a special communion with God that ought to be honored?

Hiding in plain sight

I was in Ybor City, near Tampa, Florida, at a bar that smelled of Cuban cigars and vibrated with Cuban music. It felt like home—so much so that I stayed until 10:30 one night. A tableful of young men and women sat down next to me. It was as though they only came out of the shadows at night.

To say these young people were tattooed doesn't come close to describing the number, volume, and character of their tattoos. They were covered from head to toe. Even on their faces and shaved heads. After months of research I'd started bumping into a community of people—like these—that only come out at night because their appearance is too shocking, even by today's standards. Like the time I met the group of guys outside the seafood restaurant in Maryland, I felt like I'd hit the mother lode.

Imagine that scene from *Raiders of the Lost Ark* where Indiana Jones reads hieroglyphics with a torch to find clues about the location of the Ark of the Covenant—I felt kind of like that. But I didn't want to become overwhelmed by the moment, or overwhelm them. These were my own kids' ages—in their 20s—so I automatically liked them, and in some strange way I wanted to father and encourage them. But to be honest, although I hoped I could engage them, I was afraid too. This was no time to launch into a happy-happy "Hey, I'm Al the tattoo-researcher guy, and I'm ready to know if you're ready to tell!"

I sat for about 20 minutes before turning to say hello. They didn't respond. After all, at least in appearance, I certainly wasn't their kind—an older white guy in a pressed white shirt, shiny loafers, and geeky glasses. But I persisted, not taking their silence as a message to stop, even thought that could have been exactly what they were saying.

"I'm researching tattoos and I was wondering if you could help me for just a few minutes."

"It's a free country. Go ahead and ask your questions, mister," came the response from the oldest, maybe 30-ish guy on the opposite side of the table.

"You have a lot of tattoos. Why?"

"Why not?"

As I looked, but tried not to stare, I saw one guy had implants that made horns on his head. Another one looked like a cat and had whiskers tattooed on him. Another had what looked like images of demons skewering each other with swords. Another had a tattoo of a flaming ghost skull riding a motorcycle to what looked like hell. These precious youth could only find company with like kind.

"We don't see the world like you do, and we don't mind telling you that," said one of the girls.

"What do you see?" I asked.

"It's hell, so why not just say it out loud, man!" said the cat-tattooed guy.

"Can I ask you a hard question?"

No one jumped to answer.

"Do you guys have jobs?"

"Of course we do!"

"Where do you work?"

"We work night shifts."

One did paperwork at a cab company, another worked at a tattoo studio, and another worked in his mom's floral business in the back, arranging flowers. The other three didn't answer.

"Help me understand you," I said. "No disrespect meant, really. I have kids that are your age and you kind of remind me of them."

The demon-horned guy spoke up. "Just because we chose another world doesn't mean yours is better; I tried your world and it's phony. These are my friends and family for life. We look out for each other and do whatever is needed when one of us needs help."

"So your tattoos bond you?"

The quietest guy in the bunch suddenly opened up. "Look, we know we don't fit in, and frankly, we don't want to. If God made this f**king planet, then He can kiss my a**. We can't change the wrongs done to us, and the things we did in return."

"Do you think there is a God?" I asked.

"If there is, He has a lot to answer for," said the horned guy.

Doing tattoo research comes with knowing when to move on. I felt like my time was up.

"It was a pleasure meeting you." I shook everyone's hand. "God bless you," I said.

A girl with sad eyes replied, "God bless you."

As I drove away, I thought about God's question to Adam in the garden of Eden. Remember, this was after he and Eve had eaten the forbidden fruit. When they did they were suddenly ashamed and embarrassed. When God showed up to hang out with them he found Adam and Eve hiding, as if they could keep God from seeing them.

God said, "Where are you?" Wow, what a question! Adam and Eve were now painfully aware that … well, in the words of the night freaks in Ybor City, "We can't change the wrongs done to us, and the things we did." The weight of the curse they had unleashed was pressing in on their souls, creating unbearable pain.

"Where are you?"

Adam answered, "When I heard You in the garden I was afraid because I was naked and hid myself."

Could Adam's answer be the first instance in history of a soul covering its pain from a self-inflicted wound? Could the external tattoo be a sign of the soul's internal rupture? How many of us fear that we've already forfeited the best in life and can never, ever get it back? How many of us cope by doing the best we can with what we've got, piecing together the fragments of our lives with others who've suffered like us—accepting that the best we'll ever know is our struggle in the wild, though every one of us longs for the garden where we started?

Resurrection and redemption

I was in Seattle, doing a conference for a church in Tacoma, Washington. One afternoon I took a walk near Pike Place, Pier 63, and on over to Myrtle Edwards Park. Along the water, I ran into a man named Eddie. He and his dog were having a great day. I stopped and asked Eddie if I could pet his dog because I was missing mine. We got talking and he began to tell me his story. As I listened I wrote it down.

I asked Eddie if I could interview him on video. He agreed, and his story continued to unfold. He was once CEO of an aluminum beam company. His life fell apart when he stopped taking his psych medications and his mental struggles worsened. He lost his job, his house, his wife, and was just now starting to talk to his kids again. He lived in his truck. He knew just where to park, he said, which I thought was a strange detail. But as he did, he pointed to my car which at that moment was being ticketed!

I returned to my interview with Eddie after being gifted with an $80 parking ticket. I saw that he had some tattoos and so I asked him about them.

"Oh," he said. "You haven't seen anything yet."

Most people who are tattooed are not ashamed of them. On the contrary, they're very proud of them, and Eddie was more than proud. He spoke like a guy buffing up his '66 Mustang at a hot-rod show. He took his shirt off and turned around. On his back was a larger-than-life hand giving the middle finger to God in Heaven!

"What do you think of that, Mr. Al? Seen anything like that before? I got it a long time ago, when everything had fallen apart."

I was taken aback, but after having been with the tattooed folks that only come out at night, nothing really shocks me anymore. Well, not much.

Eddie told me the story of his search for God and how he had asked God to speak to him, to show up in his life. After that, he said God started sending messages in his dreams. That led him to work in a shelter for homeless men and to be their chaplain. Eddie read the Bible and talked about it as he tried to help the people around him. Along the way, he said, he came to peace with God and now works for Him.

"The tattoo can't be taken off," he said. "But it reminds me of where a lot of people are with God."

Eddie's like a lot of us. We make bold declarations in response to life's wild ride, and then something happens to change us. Sometimes tattoos are sign posts that mark the places where the soul has been.

Doubting Thomas

Thomas, one of Jesus' disciples, mentioned in John chapter 20, was my kind of guy. History has dubbed him "Doubting Thomas," but I think we should call him "Just-Like-Us Thomas." He gets a bum rap for not buying into the story that Jesus beat death and emerged from the grave three days after he died. Thomas told the other disciples, "Look, unless I see the nail marks in His hands and put my finger where the nails were, and put my hand into his side, I will not believe." (John 20:25)

A week after Thomas made his bold declaration of doubt, Jesus appeared again. This time the disciples were hidden in a place where they had barred the door, so no one could enter. Jesus passed right through it. Once inside their hiding place, he showed himself to them all. Then Jesus spoke directly to Thomas, extending a personal invitation that he couldn't refuse: "Put your finger here; see my hands. Reach out your hand and put it into my side. Stop doubting and believe." Thomas said to him, "My Lord and my God!" (John 20:27-28)

Essentially, Jesus told Thomas, "Touch my tattoos, man! They're real."

Thomas did, and was dumbfounded. Here was life after the worst possible death. Here was hope after his world had been shattered. Here was the fulfillment of everything his heart ever hoped for. Jesus entered the most secret and well-protected hideout his followers could find, to find the friend who was most hidden from him.

It's for you

If he wanted, God could write messages in the sky—and sometimes he does. God could send messages in dreams, and he does that too. And it seems God also sends special messages using tattoos. He's certainly done that with me in the exchanges I've been privileged to share, meeting so many precious souls.

But God also chose—and I can't seem to get around it—to write a message on Jesus' skin! The marks that Thomas touched are the marks that put to death the ultimate power of death for every human soul. The nail prints in his hands and feet, the gash from the spear that was thrust in his side, the marks on his scalp from the thorny crown, and the field of furrowed flesh on his back—all are the tattoos that illustrate the depth of passion God has for us.

And the message of Jesus' tats?
- You were intended to live in the garden
- You long to be whole
- You're wounded and can't put yourself back together again
- You believe it's too late for anything but making the best out of what you have
- I wear your story
- I am you story
- Your trauma is my tattoo
- I am the answer to the secrets of your soul
- Because of this, one day you will be with Me in paradise

Thousands of years before Jesus' birth, a shaman called Isaiah foretold the story of Jesus and the meanings of his marks. Here's my translation of Isaiah's prediction:

He was despised and rejected by everyone; a man of sorrows and acquainted with grief. Seeing this many hid their faces from him because his condition was so abhorrent to look at. He was despised by everyone, no one held him in any esteem whatsoever. He was shunned.

But it's absolutely certain that he bears our griefs and carries our sorrows. How could this be anything other than the unmistakable evidence that God himself afflicted Jesus? Who else could possibly carry the weight of this world!

He was wounded as a result of what has broken and disabled all of us. He was bruised because of everything in us that is at war with who we are, and what we were created to be; everything about us that we want to hide from ourselves. And yet, the consequence of our inescapable, tortured dilemma was laid upon him, not us!

In fact, unable to do anything to fix ourselves, he took it all, everything, on himself. Imagine that the totality of all human wounding, evil, suffering, and responsibility for it, was laid on him!

By his stripes, by his marks, by his torn flesh, we are healed! At one time or another we've all gone astray; and we've all tried to fix ourselves, or have given up trying, not caring anymore. Every one of us has tried to save ourselves; and yet—this is impossible to believe—God laid what is clearly our responsibility for our screwed up, messed up, always falling short lives, on him, on Jesus! And without a whimper he took it. He took it all!

And when God saw that his Son's sacrifice of bearing what we find unthinkable was complete, he was relieved that all the souls he has lovingly created would never again risk the loss of paradise—if we will see and honor, if we will respect and embrace the suffering he has received in himself, so we might be free.

(Isaiah 53)

Jeremiah Denton blinked in Morse code, messaging the word T-O-R-T-U-R-E through the lens of his captor's camera; it was a brilliant, heroic, and possibly life-threatening action. But he couldn't free himself from prison. When Jesus shouted "My God, My God, why have you forsaken me?" as he hung on the humiliating cross he was speaking for all of humanity, crying out on every soul's behalf. He was not simply in solidarity with our suffering; it was much more than that: He endured torture to spare us from it. By his stripes—by his suffering, by his death that conquered death—we are freed to live in faith. Our suffering is not futile, because God's got our back.

I believe that by the stripes, the marks on Jesus' skin, God intends for all of us to be healed. Yes, it was mankind that bruised and cut Jesus. But I believe God used this incident—on purpose—to accept Jesus' self-sacrifice for every soul who receives it.

To my dear tattooed friends—I'd like to say: God does hear you, he sees the meaning beneath your tattoo, no matter what it is. Whether it's hurt, anger, profanity, hate, or self-condemnation, it has been heard in heaven. It is lodged in the wounds of Jesus. It has been owned by God Himself in the unbelievable sacrifice Jesus has already completed for you.

Can I urge you to be patient with life, with yourself, and with Him? He has a way of hiding His thoughts—that are time released— in the deep chasm of our souls; your tattoos are tethered to the secrets that live there.

Can God show up in your tattoo? I think so. I've seen it happen. Remember, two skins are talking here, not just yours.

Right: While photographing another subject, Mark Thompson, President of the Suncoast Blues Society, rolled up his sleeve and showed me his tiger tattoo. As the story goes, a friend challenged him to get a buddy tattoo if the Chicago Bulls won the championship three years in a row. They did.

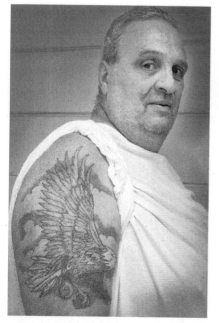

Left and above: This large man sports tattoos on his body that range from the funny to glorious.

Facing page: This summer he plans to have this mural, which he drew himself, tattooed across his back.

Chapter 10: Do You Hear What I Hear?

There's a lot of difference between listening and hearing. —G.K. Chesterton

*Quoted from her Facebook post, this androgynous woman
(as she describes herself) says, "You do not need approval
from anyone else and like myself we should all try
everyday to be confident with the person we have become.
We are all different and we all have something special to
offer this world.*

Researching tattoos has been a fascinating experience for me. It's an inspiring way to live because I know I'll encounter something I haven't seen before, and it's going to change me. That usually happens when I listen to what people are saying beneath and behind their words, and especially below the surface of their tattoos.

I discovered quite by accident that tattoos tell profound stories, and storytelling is healing. When we tell our stories, we validate our existence. Sometimes, when someone else is really listening, insight breaks out in the soul like the sun from behind a cloud, and healing begins. Add some empathy to your listening and it's magical.

When we connect with someone else through our story, and we know that they get it, it's as if we are invited to explore the layers of our lives that really matter. It's what a friend of mine calls *the magic of connection.* In those moments together when we are delving deep, we can feel our souls connecting to the Spirit.

Listening to tattoo stories has been like watching a drama powered by an invisible force. I've often felt as though I was looking over the shoulder of a surgeon who moved the soul's many chambers around to get to the spot that was covered over, hidden, and hurting. Not knowing what was in store for me or the people who literally bared their souls, again and again, I have willingly entered into what I can only describe as the holy place that lies deep inside each us.

I have come to learn that respect is everything, that stillness is everything, that anxiety-free patience is everything. I've discovered that when I am attentively observant to my heart and mind, I can be led to groundbreaking insights about my own judgments, unconscious biases, and painful confrontation with my self-righteousness. So here's a note of caution before you decide to embark on this kind of research: Get ready to see the character of your own heart. You will be shocked to discover what's there.

Whether their tattoos were seasoned or newly minted, I've discovered that most tattooed souls have a finely tuned filter set to detect the slightest presence of mockery. You must be sensitive to this and know that most people will need to check your spiritual ID before they let you in. There will be a background check; your motives and intent will be scrutinized. It's an extremely important phase during which the researcher must submit to testing and examination. If you are willing to expose yourself to just a bit of what you will be asking of your subject, then you are likely to be invited to hear stories you never thought possible.

This journey is not for the wannabe researcher or the faint of heart. You are very likely to find yourself exposed to things you don't have categories to measure—including the junk in your own soul. So if you are curious, willing, and able to ask someone about their tattoo, it helps to recognize that your connection rides on the rails of respect for the other person and acknowledgment of your own neatly tucked-away judging spirit. Allowing your soul to be still and quiet enough to listen might be the larger contest. But if you can be patient during long, awkward pauses, you may unearth buried treasure that surprises you— and sometimes even the tattoo owner.

It's in the Bible

Sometimes people take what they read in scripture at face value. But context, dear friends, is everything. If you don't understand the context it's easy to draw wrong conclusions. In the Old Testament, revered as God's word by Jews and Christians alike, Leviticus 19:28 reads: "Do not cut your bodies for the dead or put tattoo marks on yourselves. I am the Lord." God was instructing his chosen people, the new nation of Israel, to set themselves apart. They were not to imitate pagan religious practices that used cuttings or tattoos to honor the dead or as an offering to false gods.

God forbade these markings because they reflected a belief that the dead could intercede (plead with God or advocate) for the living. To conclude, as some do, that this passage prohibits modern tattoos is to misread it. Most of the people I've talked to are neither Jewish nor Christian, so that even if it was a divine prohibition, most of the folks I know wouldn't realize it. It makes no difference. Like refugees overrunning borders, tattoos have overrun the dictates of the general public. It's happening whether society thinks it should or not.

Whether you accept my explanation or not, know this: inside my heart, close to the surface, you will find me very defensive and protective of my tattooed friends. The last thing they want or need is someone writing them off or invalidating their experiences without any knowledge of who they are and what they are saying with their tattoos. These dear people have let me into their lives, becoming far more than curious specimens to be examined. They are people, like you and me.

People with lives and stories and souls as precious to God as yours. I've come to love and care about them. Any condemnation of them and their tattoos will face a strong, protective defense from me.

Let me gently, but directly remind you, God also said to love your neighbor, right? The truly loving course is to set our feelings aside, open our minds to new information, and our hearts to new opportunities with people who may not be like us, but whose souls are no less precious and whose stories just might reveal insight and truth about life we've never known before.

It might surprise you to discover that I don't have a tattoo. I have several scars from clumsy childhood and adulthood accidents, but no tattoos. Instead of that disqualifying me from this mission, however, I think it makes my curiosity more honest. Somebody once challenged me about this, asking if I got a tattoo what would it be.

I said, "I don't know, I never thought about it before."

Not good enough. The guy wouldn't let it go. He kept pushing my buttons. The snarky voice inside my head whispered, *Who does this little punk think he is!?*

When I finally got past my shallow self-consciousness I heard myself say, "I would write to my future grandchildren and say, 'There is no way I can love you more than I already do.'" We both got quiet.

Like the guy who challenged me, I want to ask you: If you don't have a tattoo, and even if you never get one, what would you write, what image would you choose? What inside your soul would be signaled by the art on your skin? I think my dad, who was born in 1924, probably had it right. He said that tattoos are for sailors who stop in distant ports; they want to be part of a band of brothers and defy the heavy load life brings. What distant port might your soul want you to visit? Who are your brothers? Over what heavy loads would you claim victory? Take some time to reflect on these questions, and you'll begin to hear the souls of those who walk among us with their messages inked on their skin.

The world where I live is my blues bar in DC. Well, it's not *mine*, but it's my turf, the place where I feel at home. I love this place and its patrons. I know them all, and they have become my parish. I hope it never ends. My wife and I love to swing dance with all our friends at the bar.

Sometime after I'd become a regular, one dear friend said to me, "Al, you're my confessor." What do you say to that? My response revealed what in hindsight I now understand was a curious ignorance on my part.

I said, "Diana, I'm a Protestant. All I do is protest!" I was trying to be lighthearted because, to be honest, I was confused. I didn't want to admit I didn't understand what she was saying.

Diana said, "Al, listen. I tell you all the things on my heart and in my soul. You just receive them. Can't you see? That's what you do here in the bar."

Whoa—a light went on in my head. I'm their confessor. The words shook me. I quickly realized that my cute little Protestant quip was my way of deflecting Diana because I didn't want to be somebody's priest. You know, the confessor—that's a Catholic thing, not my thing. But I couldn't undo Diana's experience. I couldn't undo what was going on between me and my peeps at the bar. I had to stop to process what she meant, and what it meant to me, for me, if I were to continue to do church in the blues bar.

Of course, I already knew there was an uncanny connection between me and the folks there, and a lot of them appreciated the encounters we had. But it hadn't registered with me how significant it was. Trust me, hearing someone say, "You're my confessor" cuts through any self-serving BS you might harbor about your own importance. After all, though I was joking with Diana when I said it, I am a card-carrying member of a theological tribe with an historical mission to identify truth and point out what isn't. (Even though that's not how my personality is packaged, that's the pedigree I come from.) The idea of listening with our soul to hear another living soul is often a secondary consideration at best.

So, when Diana told me what I was to her and the others, I began an internal remodeling project. I wanted to create a space inside of me to hear all the things people needed to say. It's small and primitive, nothing very impressive. But it has a shelf to carefully store the precious words of people who just need to tell, knowing that the one listening can simply receive.

This week I heard these words "Al, I have blood cancer." "Al, my husband left me for another man." "Al, I can't get a date. Why don't women like me?" "Al, I'm smoking pot and need to stop." And they're all lodged inside me in my listening space.

When I walk into my bar and see my people in the room, wordless sentiments fly through the air. I hear the silent question, "Al, do you have my story?"

Someone told me a few days ago "My son committed suicide." Today when I walk in he catches my eye, asking silently, "Al, remember my son? You got my story?" I look back, nod, and give a wink to say, "Hey man, I remember. I've got you bro, and I've got your story."

Afterword

Wisdom is the principal thing. So seek wisdom and get understanding. —Proverbs 4:7

It started with my waking up to the fact that people all around me are wearing tattoos. But this book is really not so much about tattoos as it is about the need of people to reveal who they are, whether they know themselves or not, and the need to be known. Like Moses who saw something no one had ever seen before, a bush that burned, but was not consumed, when I suddenly began to see tattoos, I just had to drop everything to go see what this sight is and what it means.

You might have picked up this book expecting to read the thoughts of someone who is either for or against tattoos. If that's what inspired your curiosity I hope what you have read has taken you from that starting point to the place where, like me, your interest has turned into more about the *what, why,* and *who* of tattoos.

Often when introduced to something outside of our experience, we feel compelled to decide if it is good or bad. Is it a tool or an obstacle? Will this help me or hinder me? When faced with these questions we sometimes fall victim to our emotions. Some of our firmest convictions have been assigned values of "good" or "bad" based on our feelings. We erect arguments that support those evaluations, throwing more wood on the fire of our belief. This is not reasoned understanding, but gut reaction.

Had I relied on gut reaction I would never have been able to sustain this journey. If we are to learn something new we cannot allow our emotions to determine what we think, do, and say. If we are going to understand something, and especially if we are going to understand people, we must listen to them. Listening to the soul is the work of spiritual anthropology.

Eventually I realized there was something beneath the tattoo image. I began to understand that tattoos are about people's need to reveal who they are—whether they know themselves or not—and their need to be known. So when I began to see—really see—the tattoos around me I had to drop everything to learn what they meant. And when I did, I was hooked. I had to know more.

I've learned that people who wear tattoos are not comic book characters, drunken sailors, or wild motorcycle gangbangers. They are people with stories like yours and mine. The only difference? They tell stories we might never dare utter. And there's our dilemma—being in the presence of someone willing to expose parts of life that we just don't know how to handle.

Every age is lost in the trees of its own time. We're so busy with the here and now that we can't see the forest. Are we even paying attention? Have you noticed that the forest is changing, that it has new residents, and they have different ways of living? Do we care about the things that we don't understand? Do we care that those things affect us—even if we don't acknowledge them? If we aren't paying attention, what do you suppose the cost will be? I think it will be that we discover too late the value of what it means to be alive, and the beauty of the things we should have treasured, but instead took for granted.

What are they? Intangible, nonmaterial things like character and compassion, kindness and goodness. Things like just being together as you muddle through life. Things like the righteous cause that compels the hero and heroine in each of us to fight for what is noble and true. Things like our God-given instincts to be seen, heard, and known, to be cherished, to be welcomed, and to belong. I am astonished at the depth and breadth that many in the tattoo community possess about life's intangible treasures, even as others write them off as freakish and bizarre.

Every culture has its mediators, its shamans, priests, and counselors. Today the tattoo artist has become for some the spiritual confidant whose confessional is his studio. Here he receives souls in turmoil who long to tell the tales from which they seek forgiveness, pardon, and peace. Today's pilgrims distrust the people and institutions that once held sway. But we are still desperate for grace and mercy wherever these can be found. As if standing in the great chasm of the soul, the tattoo artist listens to its sighs and moans, and with mystical insight beyond the comprehension of either artist or client, reveals its secrets on the skin. Like Jesus, these sojourners are willing to wear their stigmata, bearing witness to their lives, their identities, and the dreams they have yet to fulfill.

In my tribe I am a Christian minister, a pastor. It used to shock me that I, a descendant of the Protestant Reformation, which sought to explain spiritual reality and remove doubt of any kind, would find myself hunting for tales of the human spirit in the fallen, broken, and wounded world. But now I want to tell every seminarian preparing for ministry that if you want to know what is going on inside a person, get out into the wild; learn to read what is being written on the skin, for it is a portal to the soul you hope to serve.

I pray that you have glimpsed jewels of human experience in the stories and reflections you've read. By mining the meaning of each person's journey, we can help each other in the universal human pilgrimage: the search for God, and the far country of our home.

I've tried to move on to the next thing. I can't do it. This *is* the next thing. This is my fascination. And I am quite sure there is much more to discover about our humanity in this phenomenon. Something deeply intimate is being shown to us. Let's not miss it.

FOR MORE INFORMATION

I hope that this volume, and the work that my team of researchers and I continue to do, will inspire even more interest in this phenomenon. So here is my invitation to you— to tattoo convention, churches, colleges and universities, individuals and groups: I want to share our research methods and discoveries with you. Let me show you what is happening and my sense about why. Tattoo wearers permeate nearly every demographic. Perhaps they are the proverbial canaries in the stultifying mineshafts that have constrained and darkened the lives of so many others.

This book is being debuted at the 75th Sturgis Motorcycle Rally—the world's largest such gathering. Why? Because many of the three-quarters of a million people who will flood the town, the Badlands, and Black Hills for a week in August 2018 have chosen tattoos to tell the secrets of their souls. Our team of researchers will be listening, watching, and learning what these folks have to tell us.

Contact Dr. Allan Dayhoff at
tattoostellingthesecrets@gmail.com

About the Author

Allan Dayhoff received a Doctor of Ministry degree from Covenant Seminary in St. Louis, MO. Pastoring for over thirty years, he has become known as something of a spiritual anthropologist. His groundbreaking book, "God and Tattoos" received critical attention. This new edition, "Tattoos . . . Telling the Secrets of the Soul", expands the stories, insights and illustrations of his work to understand the tattoo phenomenon. Each year Al receives numerous invitations to tattoo conventions throughout the US and abroad. He writes, "More the 40% of Americans are writing on themselves. I want to know why. Exploring the secrets and stories hidden in, around, and under a tattoo is a quiet journey into the sacred place of a person's life. You cannot rush a tattoo to reveal its meaning. It is after all, the canvas of the soul. We accord dignity to people and the power of relationship when we dare to ask permission to know their story. But we must wait respectfully for whatever might be disclosed." Al makes his home with his wife Deb in the metro DC area where he pastors Blue Church and acts as executive director of Evangelize Today Ministries, a member church in the Presbyterian Church in America (PCA).

Want to hear more?
- Workshop: The Naked Truth About Evangelism
- Conference: How Does Faith Get Shared in this Time and Space?
- Residency Cohort: Ministers who want to study with Al Dayhoff, full or part-time.
- Books: "Church in a Blues Bar," "Tattoos," and "The Genius in Your Wound." (Coming soon: "Can We Re-find Lewis and Clark: Breaking out of the Echo Chamber")
- Consulting Services available. Contact Al at evangelizetoday@gmail.com

About the Editor

Michael DeArruda is a native of Massachusetts and was raised in the Roman Catholic Church. He did his undergraduate work in Education and Russian Language and Culture at Oral Roberts University in Tulsa, OK and Bridgewater State College in Massachusetts, earning a B.S. Ed. in 1975. In 1984 he was awarded the Master of Divinity degree from Princeton Theological Seminary and was ordained to the Ministry in the Presbyterian Church. Mike has served as a pastor to congregations in seven states.  For three years he coordinated pastoral care for internationally based missionaries. In 2014 he became the Stated Clerk of the ECO Presbytery of Florida. He's traveled extensively to five continents. Today Mike directs DeArrudaWeddings.com which provides relationship coaching, marriage preparation and wedding ceremonies. Over the past eight years he's served more than 500 couples from every part of the country and some from Canada, Mexico, and Europe. For the past two years Mike has introduced this unique approach to marriage ministry to seminarians in Moscow, Russia. Mike and his wife Amy live outside Tampa, Florida with Murphy, their rescued Westie-Cairn terrier.

About the Photographer

Lenore "Lennie" Duensing started taking pictures in 1957 when she received a Brownie camera for her eighth birthday. Today, as a freelance photographer of people, she focuses on capturing the hearts and souls of her subjects. Over the years, her photographs have appeared in numerous newspapers, magazines, and in photo exhibits.

My Photographic Tattoo Journey: It Began in a Dive Bar

I met Pastor Al Dayhoff at Ka'Tiki—a local dive bar, on a Florida beach, where my husband and go to listen to live music, dance, and have a couple of drinks. And, as a photographer, it's also a place where I get lots of interesting pictures. I'd watched Al dancing there on a few occasions and wondered who he was. Then, several months ago, I saw that he was dancing with a good friend of mine, and when they sat down at a table to take a rest, we went over and introduced ourselves. What a surprise learning that Al was an ordained Presbyterian minister, and my immediate thought was, "What's a guy like that doing in a place like this." We learned that he'd written two books—one called "Church in a Blues Bar," and the other, "God & Tattoos: Why are people writing on themselves"—and that his church was, in fact, in a blues bar near DC. I'm not sure how exactly that conversation went, but I do remember how impressed we were with Al's thoughtfulness, his compelling ideas, and, how well and carefully he listened. And, following our talk, I had the pleasure of dancing with him.

On that day, at Ka'tiki, we began our friendship and started learning about each other. From us, he learned that we were Quakers with a Buddhist bent who believed that the "Light of God" was within us all and that there were many "roads to heaven," and, that we did not identify as Christians. Shortly after that, while sharing a meal and good conversation, Al asked me to do the photographs and interview people for the revision of *God & Tattoos*, even though he knew that I did not share the theological conclusions he'd come to in the book. I, in turn, knowing that we differed on this matter, agreed quickly because I shared his curiosity about tattoos and the stories behind them and wanted to do some exploring of my own, particularly through

photographic images and brief interviews.

I had so many questions, and to be honest, I was disturbed by the ever-spreading trend of covering the skin—the body's largest and most visible organ—with tattoos. As an artist, I've always appreciated the beauty

of the human body and the many shades of color in which it's wrapped. So, what was going on, on both the personal and societal levels, that made so many people, particularly young people (representing a wide variety of socio-economic groups, educational levels, ethnic backgrounds, etc.), want to cover their skin with images that would last a lifetime? What need did they have to share their personal narratives— their memories, joys, interests, angers, and, innermost sorrows publicly? Did they do it as a personal communication with themselves, a way to declare their identities in a chaotic world, or, as a way to connect with others?

So, off I went with wild enthusiasm. I started by taking pictures of friends, family members, and acquaintances and asking them questions about the meaning of the pictures and words they'd put on their bodies. Then, I have to confess, I came to a crashing halt. I was becoming overwhelmed with the task of selecting just the right subjects, when so many people around me were "inked." Additionally, I had to choose among the many types of tattoos I was observing, which ranged from the ridiculous to the sublime (with most in between). For example, I saw a host of images of: dogs and cats (some dead, some still alive); famous cartoon characters and super heroes; flowers, butterflies, and birds; daggers and guns; badges of military service; mandalas, crosses, many versions of Jesus, and other religious symbolism. There were also lots of tattoos of voluptuous naked women on the backs, legs, and arms of both young and old men, and there were many images memorializing loved ones. I even photographed a beautiful young woman who was tattooing herself (a technique called stick and poke) and mutually tattooing with friends. She said it was a way people could bond with one another. She also said that she liked her home-made marks because they looked like prison tattoos and that gave her "an edge."

Then, of course, there was the matter of quality. The tattoos I was looking at spanned the gamut from pure artistry to absolute artistic disasters, such as the home-done one of Simba the lion my middle son got from a drunken friend when he was eighteen. He covered that one up, but has confessed he was sorry he did so because it was part of his life's story.

My first "aha" about my blockage, came not too long ago when I realized that I was not fully acknowledging my Discomfort with Al's theological assumptions. Since my deadline was approaching rapidly, I had to ask myself directly, "Am I okay completing my work on this book?" After some serious contemplation, I realized that because I so appreciated Al's storytelling, his insights, candor, and the way he respected all he interviewed, I was prepared to do this. My second "aha" was that instead of taking random photos, as I'd done when I started out, I needed to focus on the valuable stories Al was telling. From that point on, my path was clear. I knew who and what I needed to photograph to complete the job.

Now, at the end of this project, I have to say that I still don't have answers to the questions I was asking, and most likely, will continue searching for them. What I learned for sure was that almost all people have a need to tell their stories and be heard by a caring listener, and, that tattoos serve as an effective tool for opening genuine conversations. I also realized that I needed to acclimate to a new social and visual reality.

Note: the photos in this book represent my current geographical areas (Tampa Bay area, Florida, western New Jersey, and Floyd County, Virginia) and the places where we hang out (dive bars, beaches and woodlands). Most of the people included are friends, friends of our sons, and folks who we know (dancers, music lovers, and musicians) from blues and biker bars. Some were people I didn't know at all, but had a gut feeling that they would be willing subjects. I was never wrong about this. I am grateful to them all for sharing their personal stories. All of which, in some way, helped broaden my thinking. Now I'm asking people with "virgin" skin, "Why don't you have any tattoos?" But that's a subject for another photo essay.

Study Guide

Many of us feel disconnected from one another and the world around us. Well, let me invite you on a field trip outside your comfort zone. This is a 10-week study program designed for schools, social service groups, leadership teams, corporate organizations, churches, or anyone that wants a new understanding about the tattoo community. You are not required to do a tattoo interview but are encouraged to do so when you feel comfortable.

Interviews

This study is designed to help you use the characteristics of a surveyor, an architect and an engineer so that you can discover the person you who may be telling the secrets of their soul in tattoos.

Step 1: The Surveyor—discovering the tattoo.

Step 2: The Architect—laying out foundation materials through casual conversation. You'll notice from the stories in this book that most of the speaking in every encounter has come from the person I am interviewing.

Step 3: The Engineer—becoming aware of the communication barriers between you and the tattoo owner. You may quite possibly be tearing down old walls within yourself to build new bridges that will allow both you and the person you are interviewing to meet for genuine communion with one another.

Suggested opening connections for a tattoo interview

- "I like your tattoo. Does it mean something to you?"
- "What unique tattoo art! Would you mind telling me what it means to you?"
- "What a cool tattoo design! Would you mind telling me the story behind it?"
- "What a neat looking _____! What inspired you to get it?"
- "You must have found a great tattoo artist to ink your story. Mind sharing the story?"
- "Hey, great tattoo! I bet it has an even better story behind it. Care to share?"

It's important to keep the interview experience comfortable for both parties, especially when the tattoo owner is sharing the story behind the tattoo. When you ask questions, take a moment to pause and show your respect for the privilege you are being given. The goal is for you to be quiet, listening to hear what the soul is writing on the skin. You will be surprised and humbled by your discoveries. Some of the folks you interview may even let you take pictures of their tattoos. Others may not. Please remember that sharing limitations are set by the tattoo owners.

With tattoo interviews I have found there are four dominant responses:

- The tattoo owner says something/anything to get out of the situation.
- If we can respectfully stay in the conversation—not force it— the person begins to share part of the story about the tattoo.
- If we can stay in the conversation with a little bit more patience, the person may begin to interact emotionally with the tattoo.
- If we can stay in it, let the conversation flow with dignity, respect, and patience, we will observe the person interacting with the tattoo and making their own discoveries right in front of us.

Key Points:

- The goal is not to get people into your frame of mind or your set of beliefs.
- Always thank the person politely for their time and most of all, for their story.
- Shallow, false praise of someone's tattoo conveys the idea that you are a curiosity seeker, not a serious researcher. Monitor this within yourself.
- Research includes the dynamic of a tattoo or its owner giving a decoy answer. Respect and dignity . . .

Learning to be a researcher and learning to listen will take time. It's like going out into the wild on a treasure hunt and then returning to describe the emotions, thoughts, and sights to the best of your ability. When Lewis and Clark saw a buffalo all they could muster was, "It's a rock with fur."

In my research, I discovered that people don't believe anything they are told, only what they discover for themselves. Can you discover what lies under a tattoo once you do five to ten interviews of your own?

Starting with the second week the group leader will ask the following questions.

- Did anyone in your group do a tattoo interview?
- What did you discover?
- Were you able listen for the soul within their story?
- Did you sense the owner was reaching out to something or someone else, such as God?
- Did you sense the person is receiving a message from outside that is inspiring introspection and healing?

Study group directions

Designate a discussion leader. This person may open the group with a reflective comment, a meditative reading, or perhaps a paragraph from a chapter in the book to ignite conversation. Discussion leaders simply moderate the group through each of the questions, while allowing everyone to share their answers. You may not get through all the questions in your gathering and that's OK. It's important, however, to gently encourage participants to initiate tattoo interviews, share the results, and allow the group, to hear and comment on the fieldwork. Group members will make discoveries both big and small; discoveries about themselves, as well as tattoos and tattoo owners.

Godspeed, my friend.

Should you be interested in knowing more about the author, our training events, conferences, or the residency program for ministers, please contact us at
tattoostellingthesecrets@gmail.com

Chapter 1: The Canvas of the Soul

1. Did you see tattoos on someone last week?

2. What was the theme of the tattoo picture (a face, chains, watch, tiger, dragon, cartoon, skull)?

3. Where was the tattoo (shoulder, arm, leg, neck, face, head)?

4. What is your honest opinion of tattoos?

5. Does someone you care about have tattoos?

6. How do you feel about them having tattoos?

7. Have you ever been inside a tattoo studio? Why or why not?

8. Do you know how many tattoo studios are in your neighborhood?

9. What do you think are some key approaches to a successful tattoo interview?

10. Since we are only gathering information—the hidden story behind the chosen tattoo—will this be hard for you? If so, why? Will it be easy for you? If so, why?

11. Where will you find a tattoo owner? (This could be a relative, someone at a bar, on your street, your carpool, another parent at the playground, in a coffee shop, etc.)

12. Would someone like to close the session with a quotation from the book that they find inspiring?

Chapter 2: Living Tombstones

1. What is a tombstone?

2. When was the last time you visited a cemetery?

3. Where are your loved ones laid to rest?

4. How do you choose to remember your loved ones?

5. What is cremation?

6. Are you OK with cremation? (All answers are acceptable)

7. Why do you think people are tattooing the memory of their dead on their skin?

8. What are the different ways people tattoo the memory of the dead on their skin?

9. Did anyone do an interview this week?

10. Can you begin by telling us where you did an interview?

11. How you did you approach the tattoo owner?

12. Was it easy or difficult for you to approach the tattoo owner? Why?

13. What story did you find on/under their skin?

14. How did their story make you feel?

15. Were you able to relate to their story? If so, how?

16. What do you think about the tattoo owner now that you've heard the story behind their tattoo?

17. Would someone like to close the session with a quote from the book that they find inspiring?

Chapter 3: Poetry in Motion

1. What is a poem?

2. What's hidden inside line and verse?

3. Can spiritual truths be captured in poetry? How have you experienced this?

4. Do you have a favorite poem?

5. If so, what is the poem about?

6. Why do you think people are writing poetry on their skin?

7. What are possible forms of the tattoo poetry?

8. Did anyone do an interview?

9. Can you begin by telling us where you met them?

10. How did you approach your interview?

11. Was it easier or harder this week?

12. How did it make you feel?

13. What type of poetry did you find in the tattoo?

14. What type of poetry did you discover in the soul of the owner?

15. What was unique about this tattoo interview?

16. Would someone like to close the session with a quote from the book that inspires you to try asking someone, "I like your tattoo. Does it mean something?"

Chapter 4: Weaponize Me

1. Can you describe a man's tattoo?

2. Are men's tattoos often different from women's?

3. What weapons have you seen in men's tattoos?

4. Why do you think they do this?

5. Do weapons cover their internal wounds?

6. Do you have a son or grandson with tattoos? What are they? What do they mean?

7. Did anyone do an interview this week?

8. Can you begin by telling us where you met the owner?

9. How did you approach your interview this week?

10. Was as it easier or harder than the one before?

11. If so, how?

12. What did you discover hidden in the tattoo?

13. What did you discover in the soul of the owner?

14. How did it make you feel?

15. What key things made this week s interview successful?

16. Would someone like to close the session with a quote from the book that inspires you to try asking someone, "I like your tattoo. Does it mean something?"

Chapter 5: She Walks in Beauty

1. What is beauty?

2. Who defines beauty?

3. How do you feel about women getting tattoos?

4. Why do you think so many women are getting tattoos?

5. What are they saying to themselves and others by getting tattoos?

6. Do you have a daughter, niece or granddaughter with a tattoo?

7. If yes, what type of tattoo is it?

8. What does it mean to them?

9. What does it mean to You?

10. Did anyone do an interview this week?

11. Can you begin by telling us where you did your interview?

12. How you did you approach the tattoo owner?

13. Was it easy or hard?

14. What did you find out about the tattoo's story?

15. What did you learn about the soul wearing the tattoo?

16. How did it make you feel?

17. What are your essential key ingredients to a successful tattoo interview?

18. Would someone like to close the session with a quote from the book that inspires you to try asking someone, "I like your tattoo. Does it mean something?"

Chapter 6: Tattoos Are Totems

1. What is a totem?

2. Did God create us to think this way (are we like a hummingbird, a soldier, a philosopher, a healer, etc.)?

3. Why are people writing totems on their skin?

4. If you tattooed your totem on your skin, what would it be?

5. Did anyone do an interview this week?

6. Can you begin by telling us where?

7. How you did you approach the interview this week?

8. Was it easier or harder than last week? Why?

9. What kind of totems have you found during interviews?

10. What were your keys to a successful tattoo interview?

11. How did it make you feel?

12. Would someone like to close the session with a quote from the book that inspires you to try asking someone, "I like your tattoo. Does it mean something?"

Chapter 7: The Soul Needs Its Shaman

1. What is a shaman?

2. Why have so many left behind the traditional shaman of minister, rabbi, grandparent?

3. Why is the tattoo artist a new shaman for so many people?

4. Did anyone do an interview this week?

5. Can you begin by telling us where you were?

6. How did you approach your interview?

7. Was it easy or hard for you?

8. What stories did you find within the tattoo and the owner?

9. How did the story make you feel?

10. What were your key aspects to a successful tattoo interview?

11. Would someone like to close the session with a quote from the book that inspires you to try asking someone "I like your tattoo. Does it mean something?"

Chapter 8: The Language of Recovery

1. What is a recovery tattoo?

2. What are people recovering from?

3. What kind of recovery is going on in your family or network of people?

4. Why are people putting their recovery on their skin?

5. Do you think the tattoo helps in the process of recovery?

6. Did anyone do an interview this week?

7. Can you begin by telling us where you were?

8. How did you approach your interview this week?

9. Was it easy or hard?

10. What story did you discover about the tattoo and the owner?

11. How did it make you feel?

12. What were your key ingredients to a successful tattoo interview?

13. Would someone like to close the session with a quote from the book that inspires you to try asking someone, "I like your tattoo. Does it mean something?"

Chapter 9: It's Not Just Your Skin Talking

1. What do you think about God using tattoos to communicate?

2. What messages do you think God wrote on Jesus?

3. Have you discerned that there is any kind of spiritual communication being received by a person through their tattoo or being made by a person through their tattoo? Can you talk about that?

4. Do you think there will be marked skin in heaven?

5. Did anyone do an interview?

6. Can you begin by telling us where you met the tattoo owner?

7. How did you approach the tattoo owner?

8. Was it easy or hard for you?

9. What stories did you find within the tattoo and the owner?

10. How did it make you feel?

11. What are your key ingredients to a successful tattoo interview?

12. Would someone like to close the session with a quote from the book that inspires you to try asking someone, "I like your tattoo. Does it mean something?"

Chapter 10: Do You Hear What I Hear?

1. What changed you and your point of view through this adventure?

2. Is there anything confusing, puzzling or troubling to you?

3. If you got a tattoo what would it be?

4. Has your view of the tattoo culture changed?

5. Did anyone do an interview?

6. Can you begin by telling us where you met the tattoo owner?

7. How did you approach the tattoo owner?

8. Was it easy or hard for you?

9. What unique stories did you discover within the tattoo and the owner?

10. How did it make you feel?

11. What are your key ingredients to a successful tattoo interview?

12. Would someone like to close the session with a quote from the book that inspires you to try asking someone, "I like your tattoo. Does it mean something?"